WHAT SEEMS IMPOSSIBLE

LIVING EVERYDAY IN THE POWER OF POSSIBILITY

SCOTT JOHNSON

HARRISON HOUSE PUBLISHING

All scripture is taken from the *New International Version,* unless otherwise noted.

ISBN: 978-160683-422-0

What Seems Impossible
Living Everyday in the Power of Possibility
© 2011 Scott Johnson

Published by Harrison House Publishing
Tulsa, OK 74145

DEDICATION

To Mom and Dad who first taught

me the power of possibility.

CONTENTS

Foreword 1

Introduction.. 3

1 **That Doesn't Make Sense!**... 5
But it sure does make faith.

2 **Strategies Designed To Make Faith**............................ 21
They are the doors to your success.

3 **Clear Out Relational Hostility** 37
Before it steals your faith.

4 **Mix Faith & Wisdom Now**... 45
Learn how to be a "today's believer" to produce a better tomorrow.

5 **Conquer Your Airspace** 65
Then you'll win the war on the ground.

6 **God Gets You!** 81
He understands you and has personal answers.

7 **Transition—No Man's Land**..................................... 97
God's ways to get you through change.

8 **Simplify Your Life—But Stay In Motion**.............. 103
Navigating between "Go" and "You've arrived."

9 **Listen To The Messenger** 119
God has one for you.

10 **Make The Switch** 135
Learn to think God's thoughts.

11 **Express Your Faith** 141
And make it grow.

12 **Trust God—No Matter What** 153
And He will honor your faith.

13 **Our Call To Action** 171
Whatever He tells you to do, do it!

Endnotes 187

Appendix I 195

Appendix II 197

About the Author 199

FOREWORD

This is a good book!

In the introduction Scott said, "My goal in the pages of this book is to so demonstrate for you the power of possibility way of living, that you are inspired to reach for it, embrace it and live it to the fullest. My goal is to show you through the power of a mature relationship with God you can learn to use your faith to prevent future problems—as well as fix your existing ones." Well, I believe he has, with God's anointing, done just that.

I know you and I both have been up against what seemed to be overwhelming circumstances. That's when we said, "What am I going to do?"

Think about it. What if someone answered and said, "Do this!" Wow! A plan. Something I can carry out now to release the faith that will deliver me from this MESS. Action! Like when Scott led a young man to step over lines they had drawn in the carpet. Each step a step of faith. Each step away from the "giant" that held this man in bondage and each step a step toward Jesus and great victory. That one story of God's great love is worth reading the whole book. Why? Because God is no respecter of persons. God's Word works. It works every time it's put to work in faith. That was a simple strategy from heaven's plan that released faith in God. How exciting is that?!

Take the time to read and reread *What Seems Impossible*. Look up the scriptures. Faith comes by hearing and hearing by the Word of God—read and listen. Read and believe it. Read and act. Step over the lines of faith. Jesus is always there—arms open, smiling and saying, "You can do it!"

Come on. All things are possible to him who believes.

JESUS IS LORD!

–Kenneth Copeland

2

INTRODUCTION

We love hearing stories of heroic actions, miraculous rescues and winning against all odds. We long to be a part of something huge and meaningful—and feel the thrill of overcoming and conquering. We feel so satisfied with movies where the underdog always wins. We feel complete when we make a difference in a person's life or serve our community in a charitable way.

God made us that way. He made us to live above the challenges of life and see things in a hopeful and positive way. He made us to be the hero in the movie and have everything turn out right. He made us capable of changing and helping others change and grow. He made us to hunger to see the impossible in everyday life. He made us with an innate desire to see seemingly impossible barriers broken.

But life has a way of throwing curve balls at us—of lying to us that we can't—and all too often, we buy into that lie, and live defeated. Yes, things happen—tragic things we never planned for or saw coming. But God never meant for any of that to keep us down.

There is a way to overcome, and win—every time. There is a way to break through the ceilings we find pressing down on us. There is a way to live whole, happy and surrounded by great friends and family. There's a way to live prosperous and healthy, no matter how bleak things look. There is a way to live emotionally charged with optimism and expectation every day.

I call this way *experiencing the power of possibility.*

My goal in the pages of this book is to so demonstrate for you the power of possibility way of living, that you are inspired to reach for it, embrace it and live it to the fullest. My goal is to show you through the power of a mature relationship with God you can learn to use your faith to prevent future problems—as well as fix your existing ones.

As you read many of my real-life encounters with God that have forever been imprinted in my mind and heart, you'll see how God is not just a figure I've read about in the Bible. My relationship with Him has been made real through experiences with Him—and they produce what I need and desire in my life and ministry.

That's what God's plan is for you. It's what Jesus expects for you, and it's the Holy Spirit's creative design for your life.

It's the power of possibility. It's how you can live so that what seems impossible in your life can suddenly become possible! This is God's quest for you. It's a journey of a lifetime full of adventure and joy. I began mine as a young boy...and I'm still living it today...

–Scott Johnson

CHAPTER 1

THAT DOESN'T MAKE SENSE!

BUT IT SURE DOES MAKE FAITH

One day, when I was just a teen, I came home from school, went to the kitchen to get a snack, and heard a knock on the front door. No one else in the family was answering the door, so I opened it to find a gentleman who said he wanted to talk to my parents. I went to the backyard to get my dad. He was an evangelist at the time with nowhere to preach.

I, being the Curious George® that I am, decided to hang out and see what the man wanted. Dad invited the man in and asked Mom to serve them some iced tea. As they sat in the living room talking, I discovered that he was our landlord, we were two months behind on rent—and he wanted his money.

When he explained to Dad the reason for his visit, my dad looked him in the eye and told him the money was on its way. Now, my parents did not have any facts or information to back up that statement. They had no certainty, just their trust in God to meet all their needs, and an intuitive knowing that the answer would come that day. Today, I know what they did is called faith.

As the two sat there and drank glasses of tea, they concluded their small talk. Dad asked the landlord if he wanted some more tea, but he simply replied, "No, just rent money."

My dad calmly told him again, "The money will be here any minute."

The next few moments were very awkward. You could have cut the atmosphere with a knife. But suddenly without notice, there was another knock on the door.

Dad opened it, and there stood a gentleman who proceeded to tell my dad who he was, and that he had been praying the Lord would direct his steps. And as the story goes, the Lord directed him right to our house, straight to our front door! How odd is that? It didn't make sense.

As they continued to talk, my dad invited the gentleman in and told my mom they needed more tea. While they enjoyed the conversation, the landlord grew more anxious. The visitor was a believer, but still a complete stranger. I had never seen him before in my life.

"Again, I say to you, that if two of you agree on earth about anything that they ask, it shall be done for them by My father who is in heaven."

Matthew 18:19

The stranger said to my dad, "God sent me here for a reason," and then he asked my father what he needed. Dad introduced the stranger to the landlord and then told the stranger that we owed the landlord two months of rent. The man pulled out his checkbook, wrote out a check for the full amount we owed, and handed it to our landlord. He then asked if he could give my mom some money. So he then wrote her a check for $50 and told her to go buy something for herself.

How did that happen? How did this complete stranger know? How could this possibly be true?

GOD. GOD. GOD.

It didn't make sense! But it sure did make faith.

With God, although it seems like life's circumstances are impossible at the time, there is always the power of possibility—which is faith. My dad and mom used their faith to believe for the answers they needed. The gentleman used his faith to live for God and respond to the direction of God to go and bless my parents. These events were nothing short of a relational exchange between God and

Imagine living in faith to the extent you never need a bailout or a miraculous cure? You can live that way! We all can. But we have to learn how.

people. They didn't make sense to our natural way of thinking, but they definitely made faith—the faith necessary for my parents to get their answer, and for the stranger to get to be a blessing.

My parents knew how to use their faith to believe God for a miracle in a tight spot. I've had to do this, too. Maybe you have as well. And while my parents' experience was an amazing, miraculous moment in their Christian journey, there is something much better than needing a miracle.

It's NOT needing one!

Imagine living in faith to the extent you never need a bailout or a miraculous cure? You can live that way! We all can. But we have to learn how.

My goal in the pages of this book is to so demonstrate for you the power of possibility way of living, the power of a mature relationship with God that you learn to use your faith to prevent future problems—as well as fix your existing ones.

As you read many of my real-life encounters with God that have forever been imprinted in my mind and heart, you'll see how God is not just a figure that I've read about in the Bible. No my relationship with Him has been made real through experiences with Him—and they produce what I need and want in my life and ministry.

That's what God desires for you. It's what Jesus yearns for you, and it's the Holy Spirit's purpose for your life as well.

It's the power of possibility. It's how you can live so that what seems impossible in your life can suddenly become possible! This is God's quest for you. It's a journey of a lifetime full of adventure and joy. I began mine as a young boy...and I'm still living it today...

THE POWER OF POSSIBILITY—FOR EVERY PART OF YOUR LIFE

It was a cool autumn Sunday morning in our little, quiet Texas town. I was just a 10-year-old, and my dad had become a preacher in recent months. His career change had carved out a new season for our family. When Mom woke me up, I was running a temperature and feeling lousy. The flu bug had hit me bad.

Dad was already at the church, so Mom told me it would be all right to just stay in bed, and she'd see me after the service. We lived just a few yards away from the church in a parsonage—a home next door to the church or built onto the structure of the church. Living in the parsonage was a great privilege, but definitely felt odd whenever you had a funeral, and that night you found you were sleeping with a casket in the same house that you were in…strange.

I don't remember anything about the rest of that day. I must have slept through most of it until that evening when I awoke about an hour before the Sunday evening service. Dad came into my room, and I was still running a fever. So he prayed for my healing—and nothing changed.

My goal in the pages of this book is to so demonstrate for you the power of possibility way of living, the power of a mature relationship with God that you learn to use your faith to prevent future problems— as well as fix your existing ones.

"Scott," he said, "I poured a glass of milk for you. It's in the kitchen on the table. If you'll get dressed, drink that milk, and come over to the service, I believe God will heal you. Do you believe, Scott?"

*Maybe when I **agree** with him, I'll be healed,* I thought.

"Yes sir, I believe." But still, in the natural, nothing happened.

"Now it's up to you," he said, and off he went to church.

After he left, I didn't feel any better—I felt worse. The flu had taken all my energy. I was still burning up with fever, coughing consistently, and my head felt stopped up.

OK, Lord, I'm getting up! I said in my mind as I got up and got dressed. Still, nothing happened.

I could hear that the song service had already started. The people's singing carried across the lawn to the parsonage…

This is my story…

This is my song…

Praising my savior all the day long…[1]

I went in the kitchen and looked at that milk. "Oh, Lord, I'm gonna drink this milk!"

What I haven't told you yet is that I hate milk—and not only do I hate milk, but also I hate its texture and its taste, too! It's white for Pete's sake! Just like mayonnaise! And I don't like mayonnaise either! To be clear, just in case I haven't been clear enough, there is absolutely nothing I like about milk! In fact, later as an adult, I learned I was lactose intolerant. Subconsciously, maybe my body knew that all along and wanted me to reject it back then!

The Bible is full of stories that just don't make sense to the natural mind, but to God, they are the perfect plan.

But, I had been raised to understand how to behave in faith, how to walk by faith, and how to release my faith. So, I prayed over the milk—all the while hoping God would heal me quickly so I wouldn't have to drink it—and I drank it. For the next 5 minutes—OK, 10 minutes—I forced myself to drink every last drop of that glass of milk. As I did, again I thought, *Maybe when I finish it, I'll be healed.* Nothing happened. Nothing changed.

I walked over to the church, reached to open the door and thought again…*Maybe here God will see my faith and heal me before I ever go in.* I continued to open the door and step inside the foyer, but nothing happened. Nothing changed in how I felt.

Well, maybe when I get into the sanctuary, maybe that's when my healing will happen.

Nope. I opened the doors, stepped in and stopped. I was feeling so nauseous. I had cold sweats. I wasn't getting any better! I was growing worse!

I walked down the aisle all the way to the front row. The congregation began singing "Jesus Is the Sweetest Name I Know,"[2] and I joined in with them.

By the time we sang the chorus the second time, I noticed I wasn't sick any longer. The power of possibility had been released into my body, and I was experiencing it firsthand as a 10-year-old kid.

Since that day, not only have I been healed countless times, but also hundreds of others have been healed through the power of possibility in my life and ministry. The stories are too numerous to list in one book, but needless to say, the same God who revealed himself to a 10-year-old preacher's kid has been doing the seemingly impossible in my life for decades now. He is the same God I encountered when Dad told me to drink a glass of milk, and come on over to the service. I stepped out in faith, and God's power of possibility was increased in my life. Looking back, I'm not sure what took more faith—drinking the milk or walking through the church doors!

GOD'S STORIES OF WHAT'S POSSIBLE

I've told you two of God's stories from my life, now let me tell you one of God's from the Bible. They are amazing stories of faith!

Several men were out chopping wood one day with their preacher (Elisha) because they were building him a house. As they were chopping, the sun beat down on them and sweat dripped from their brows. One of the men lifted the axe overhead, swung it with all his strength, and the axe head flew off and splashed into a nearby river.

The man watched in horror and shouted, "Preacher! Preacher! The axe head fell off and went into the river! I have to get it! It's not mine—it's borrowed! What am I going to do?"

The preacher had sympathy on this young man and walked over to a tree, broke off a limb, and tossed it into the river. As all the men were watching, they were thinking, *What on earth is that preacher doing now? Why is he tossing a stick in the water? That makes no sense at all.*

As the stick hit the surface of the water, something jumped up and began to float.

What was it?

Could it be?

*No, surely it wasn't…*but it was!

The axe head was floating toward the bank of the river.

Now that is impossible! We all know that iron doesn't float. It just doesn't make sense, but it's a true story that made faith.[3]

The Bible is full of stories—facts recorded over time that seem impossible. They are stories of people's problems and dilemmas, all resolved with heavenly results that just don't make sense. But they

We all love hearing these kinds of stories about Elijah and others is because we hunger to see the impossible overcome in this dead-end world. We have an innate desire to see what seems like impossible barriers broken.

make faith. To God, they are the perfect plan. He leads us this way on purpose so we won't rely on what we can figure out, but rather we will rely completely and totally on Him in faith.

When Daniel was in the lion's den and should have been eaten, he came out unharmed. It didn't make sense—but it made his faith stronger, and it creates faith in us to this day.[4]

Lifting a rod and expecting a sea to part didn't make sense either, but when Moses did it, the children of Israel walked across the Red Sea on dry ground.[5] It strengthened their faith in God and builds faith in us.

One of my favorite stories is when the whole land was in a famine and Elijah was hanging out at the Brook Kerith where God had been sustaining him by sending ravens with food every day.[6] But the brook dried up and God told Elijah it was time to go to town where he would meet a widow who would provide food for him.

Elijah got to town, and sure enough, there was a widow gathering sticks. He asked her for a drink.

Well, I guess I can do one last nice thing before I die, she thought.

So she heads off to get water when Elijah stops her and asks, "While you're at it, could you make lunch and bring it back?"

What is this preacher thinking? We are in the middle of a famine, people are dying all around us and he wants me to fix him lunch? I don't even have enough food to keep my boy and me alive!

Can you hear her thinking?

"As surely as the Lord your God lives," she replied, "I don't have any bread—only a handful of flour in a jar and a little oil in a jug. I am gathering a few sticks to take home and make a meal for myself and my son, that we may eat it—and die."

Elijah said to her, "Don't be afraid. Go home and do as you have said. But first make a small cake of bread for me from what you have and bring it to me, and then make something for yourself and your son. For this is what the Lord, the God of Israel, says, 'The jar of flour will not be used up and the jug of oil will not run dry until the day the Lord gives rain on the land.'"[7]

Did I hear him right? That is ridiculous. Who has ever heard of such a thing? The jar of flour will not be used up—that doesn't make any sense! But…he is the man of God…

"She went away and did as Elijah had told her. So there was food every day for Elijah and for the woman and her family. For the jar of flour was not used up and the jug of oil did not run dry, in keeping with the word of the Lord spoken by Elijah."[8]

It sure didn't make sense, but it made faith!

YOUR MIND—THE FIRST OBSTACLE TO WHAT'S POSSIBLE

The reason we all love hearing these kinds of stories about Elijah and others is because we hunger to see the impossible overcome in this dead-end world. We have an innate desire to see what seems like impossible barriers broken, but we have something working against us—our minds.

I can't do that because I don't have enough money. I don't know the right people. I'm just never going to get a break. Yes, I know they did it, but that's them. They're smart, tall and good-looking. You just don't know me. I take two steps forward just to wind up going four steps back.

The eternal realm. It's the place where the Spirit of God lives, and it is in that realm with all its power where we can change our circumstances and situations supernaturally. It's where the power of possibility originates.

The mind is our first obstacle to overcoming what seems impossible. Our minds are conditioned to the failure of the man-made system of this realm. Our thinking is trained for natural progression, so we think to get to point F, we must start at point A, working our way through points B, C, D and E. But there is a parallel universe out there—an unseen realm—that is in existence right alongside this natural realm. The Bible calls it the eternal realm. It's the place where the Spirit of God lives, and it is in that realm with all its power where we can change our circumstances and situations supernaturally. It's where the power of possibility originates. It's the place that makes it possible to go from point A to point E in one step.

So we have to look beyond the realm in which we live. We have to look to this eternal realm: "So we fix our eyes not on what is seen, but on what is unseen, because what is seen is temporary, but what is unseen is eternal."[9]

Have you ever seen a spirit? Whether you have or haven't doesn't matter. Spirits do exist in the unseen, eternal realm. In fact, the Bible tells us that God is spirit, and His worshipers must worship in spirit and in truth.[10]

The word *worship* in this scripture actually means "work." So we could say it this way: "God is spirit and lives in an invisible reality—an eternal reality—and those who work with Him must work with Him in spirit and in truth."

Paul also told us that we are spirit, we have a soul (mind, will and emotions) and we live in a body.[11] This means that as a believer, your life should look different than that of an unbeliever. You are not empowered by Wheaties® alone, regardless of what you see on TV. The Bible says that a strong spirit will sustain a man, even in sickness.[12] But how is the spirit sustained? How is it strengthened?

Paul also told us that we are spirit, we have a soul (mind, will and emotions) and we live in a body.

As a believer, your spirit receives power and energy from a different source—it comes from God, from a parallel world, that eternal realm. That is why He says, "Not by might nor by power, but by my Spirit,' says the Lord Almighty."[13]

When my wife, Missy, and I planted BelieversWay Church and Ministries in 1999, we hadn't even had our first service yet, when a phone call came to our offices. We had just rented office space to plan and work, and this call came a few weeks before our first Sunday morning service.

Missy, who had supervised hundreds through the years at a large international ministry, was now most of the staff. She was the front desk receptionist, accountant and office team…and did everything except preach—that was my role. It was a very funny time in our lives as we juggled to cover all the bases.

Late one afternoon, as she was manning the office, someone called panicking. They asked, "Do you believe in spirits?"

"Yes," she replied.

"Well, I'm in my bedroom and there's a blanket that is dancing, and I know it's the devil, and I'm scared to death."

All we have to do is use the power of possibility—our faith—to bring things out of God's kingdom and into ours.

Missy responded, "Well, if that's all the devil can do is make your blanket dance, you don't have anything to worry about." She laughed and, in Jesus' Name, rebuked that spirit. Immediately, the person said it fell to the floor in a heap.

He said, "You did it!"

A few weeks later, the caller attended our church service, and has been a partner with BelieversWay ever since—and one of the strongest believers I've seen.

Yes, there is a spiritual dimension.

Most of the time, when we think of "the spirit," we think of Heaven, but Jesus prayed, "Your kingdom come, your will be done on earth as it is in heaven."[14]

When Jesus came, He brought His kingdom with Him, but that kingdom is in an unseen reality and a "non-linear" dimension that is accessed by a believer's faith.

16

To help you understand what I mean by non-linear, let me explain to you how we used to do video editing years ago. (I was the director of a television ministry for years, so I've lived through many advances in technology.) To edit scene four, we first had to go through the first three scenes. It was a linear process—meaning it had to go in sequential order. But in today's technological non-linear world of editing, to edit scene four, I can simply punch a button and instantly go right to scene four, completely skipping scenes one, two and three. When non-linear editing came about, it certainly sped things up.

Or think of it this way. Before Microsoft Windows was introduced to the market, you had to completely open and close each computer screen in software programs. When Microsoft gave us "windows," we could open, close, maximize and minimize multiple computer screens all at once! There were multiple dimensions.

Another example is looking up scriptures. If you look up a scripture in your Bible, John 3:16 for instance, you thumb through to find John, then chapter 3, then you scan the page until you get to verse 16—that's linear. But if you have that scripture memorized, your brain can jump right to it and you can spout out, "For God so loved the world..." without having to think through the verses ahead of it—that's non-linear. Or you can go to a Bible website and type in the verse. It pops up and you're there! That's non-linear.

God's kingdom is in a non-linear dimension that seems impossible to our natural minds. It just doesn't make sense to our minds and linear way of thinking that the impossible can happen without this or that happening first. But it can! All we have to do is use the power of possibility—our faith—to bring things out of His kingdom and into ours.

LIVE WITH AN OPEN HEART—WHERE FAITH CAN GROW

When Missy and I began the first BelieversWay Church in Amarillo, Texas, we were meeting in a community center. We grew from 70 to 200 people in just a few months. One man who came in those early months worked in forensics for law enforcement.

One day, as we were sitting at a coffee bar talking, he told me he had terrible migraine headaches and had suffered with them for years. As he spoke, an assurance of strong faith came over me. I knew if I touched him, he would be made whole. The Bible tells us, "Lay hands on the sick and they'll recover."[15]

> *When we live with an open heart, it creates an action of generosity and so it is with God. God so loved the world He gave.*

So I reached over and grabbed his hand and spoke to the symptoms. Twelve years later, he hasn't had a migraine since.

Immediately after that experience, he began to tithe. Up until that moment, he was just a tipper. In fact, he had left his previous church because he felt like the preacher was trying to get his money. But when he began biblically tithing, he began having sizable contracts come in that tripled his income in just one year!

It is amazing how one area of a person's life affects the next. Although he was dealing with a seemingly impossible situation with migraines, when the power of possibility touched his life, it opened up his heart in thankfulness and he became generous to God in return with his finances. He no longer saw it as the preacher and God in collaboration with one another trying to get his money. It became an overflow of his relationship with God.

I believe for the first time in his life, he experienced God, and God was bigger, more powerful and compassionate than he ever thought possible. His journey up until that moment with God was a religious ritual more than anything else. When he received his healing, it changed everything. When we live with an open heart, it creates an action of generosity and so it is with God. God so loved the world He gave.[16]

God loves humanity so much, that His heart is continuously open to all of us. So generosity pours from Him constantly toward the Earth. It's real. His love is far reaching. His touch is tangible, and with it comes the power of possibility!

It is this power that is creative and restorative. It produces health and healing which do not originate in this natural dimension. True prosperity—true abundance and blessing, the rich abundance of Heaven—doesn't originate here on this level. All of these origins are in the unseen realm—the eternal realm—and by faith, we can bring health, healing, prosperity, abundance and blessing into our natural reality, possessing a heavenly outcome!

In what area of your life do you need the power of possibility? Whatever it is, God has ways—strategies—that will get it to you. All you have to do is learn to flow with Him and His ways.

CHAPTER 2

STRATEGIES DESIGNED TO MAKE FAITH

THEY ARE THE DOORS TO YOUR SUCCESS

Years ago, a young man came to me with tears in his eyes. He had come to the end of himself. Weeping, he laid his head on my shoulder and cried. A few minutes passed, and when he composed himself, he said, "I'm addicted."

"Addicted to what?" I asked.

"I'm addicted to prescription meds. Hydrocodone."

For the next several hours, we wept, he repented, we took communion, and then I drew lines on the carpet that we stepped across over and over, moving further and further away from the addiction with each step. It was a natural action we took as we prayed and declared the power of addiction broken in his life. God was present. It was an image that could be forever etched in his mind and on his heart. The change that occurred was powerful. We had experienced the power of possibility. We had experienced faith.

The Bible tells us—and life's experiences prove it to be true—that God intends for us to have a pastor, or preacher, in the midst of our lives. There are simply certain things that need the catalyst of the preacher to affect change in our personal world. In this man's life, the message I preached affected him. It encouraged his faith to believe and seek the help he so desperately needed. He was finally ready to change—and live a life of freedom.

The actions we took—taking step after step across lines I drew on the carpet with my shoe—were real to him. Those steps were a strategy from God to make faith. They helped him to see and believe and take what's rightfully his in Christ—deliverance from addiction. Taking each of those steps was walking through the door to his success.

God has strategies for you, too. They are the doors to your success.

That young man's journey, although so much different than mine, required a common ingredient—dependence on God and His word.

When I was just a kid, my mom and dad would push me to memorize scripture. One of my earliest memories of memorizing verses was: "Trust in the Lord with all your heart, lean not to your own understanding; in all your ways acknowledge Him, and He will direct your path."[1]

That young man trusted God, and he trusted me. It was a key to his believing God and getting free.

It's always been relatively easy for me to believe God. Not just believe in Him, but actually believe Him and take Him at His word. As early as I can remember, I've trusted God for protection, healing, finances, wisdom, guidance and direction for my own personal life. So it's not just a lifestyle, it's my life. It's who I am! And it has empowered me to look to God beyond myself for others.

Think about it. If I can't trust God for me, how can I trust Him for you? So by trusting Him, I bring a healthy me to every relationship, and every message. Having grown up in faith, it's easy for me. I've experienced God in all areas of my life throughout my journey. He's not an invisible God to me. He is very real to me because of our experiences together. He can be just as real to you. All you have to do is believe Him. He wants you to have faith, so you can walk through all the doors He opens for you.

GOD'S POWER CAN BE FELT

When I think of faith, I always think of Matthew 9, the story of the woman with the issue of blood. This woman was a wealthy woman before her bleeding started. How do I know this? Because she had gone all across the country going from doctor to doctor and had spent all her money trying to find a cure.

Twelve years later, she was still bleeding and becoming weaker and more anemic every day. She had no more money, but she heard a preacher preaching about Jesus, and she heard of all the signs, wonders and miracles that were happening in His ministry.

She began to wonder and tell herself that if she could just touch the hem of Jesus' garment, then she just knew she would be healed and made whole. She had to find this Jesus.

Finally, she did find out where He was and went to Him, but there was a huge crowd surrounding Him. She couldn't get close enough to see Him, much less touch Him. She pressed in, repeating to herself, *If I could just touch Him....*

In her desperation, she continued to press in through the mob, and finally got within arm's reach. She stretched out her hand and touched the hem of His clothes.

At once Jesus realized that the power of possibility had gone out from Him. He turned around in the crowd and asked, "Who touched My clothes?"

"You see the people crowding against you," His disciples answered, "and yet you ask, 'Who touched me?'"

But Jesus kept looking around to see who had touched Him. Then the woman, knowing what had happened to her, came and fell at His feet and, trembling with fear, told Him the whole truth. He said to her, "Daughter, your faith has healed you. Go in peace and be freed from your suffering."[2]

It doesn't make sense that someone could touch a piece of clothing and be healed from a condition that even the best doctors in the world could not cure. But the power of possibility was never meant to seem reasonable or make sense—it was designed by God to create faith.

It doesn't make sense that a young man and I could draw line after line in the carpet and step over them, and he could be delivered from drugs—but it did make faith. And even to this day, he remains whole from a disease called addiction.

> *It doesn't make sense that someone could touch a piece of clothing and be healed from a condition that even the best doctors in the world could not cure. But the power of possibility was never meant to seem reasonable or make sense—it was designed by God to create faith.*

It's interesting that although the crowd was pushing up against Jesus, He immediately knew something had happened. He felt her faith and the power of possibility be released from Him.

Jesus had the anointing to heal this woman. In fact, He had the anointing to heal everyone else, too. But apparently, this woman was the only one healed that day. Why was that?

In Acts 10:38, the Bible says that Jesus went around healing all that were sick and oppressed by the devil. But it also says in Mark 6:5 that in Jesus' hometown, He couldn't do any miracles except lay hands on a few sick and heal them.

So did Jesus heal all who were sick or not? What does "all" mean?

Jesus healed all who had the faith to draw their healing from Him. In His hometown, He didn't find any faith. No one was using faith to draw from the unseen reality!

Remember, Jesus felt the power leave Him when the woman touched Him. He knew her touch was different. Faith is a very real, very powerful force that can be felt.

The woman was the only one healed that particular day, because she was the only one with the faith to draw her healing from the unseen dimension into her reality.

Remember, she had been telling herself over and over that she would be healed if she touched Him, and she believed it.

GOD IS STILL HEALING TODAY

One evening, Missy and I went to the home of one of our partners for a fun-filled evening of friendship and food. When we entered the house, there was a wonderful aroma coming from the kitchen. Our hostess was such a great cook. As we stood in the kitchen talking, they mentioned a symptom that their daughter had. She had been bleeding for months. They had gone to the doctor, tried various things and received no cure.

Immediately, the mercy of God rose up on the inside of me. I asked if I could be excused and went into the living room to pray without being interrupted. This type of encounter with God had never happened to me before. After 30 minutes, the compassion of God on me was so great that I was about to explode with His presence. He was too good! I knew the power of possibility was ready to be released.

Just then their daughter arrived home from work and I asked her parents, "May I lay hands on your daughter?"

"Yes," they replied.

Missy and I laid our hands on her womb and, suddenly, the power went from me to her.

We went on and enjoyed the rest of the evening. Later that night they called and told us the bleeding had stopped. When I laid hands on her, like medicine being released into a sick patient's body, suddenly, she had experienced the power of possibility. Years later, she is still healed.

MY PERSONAL FIGHT

We gain faith in the things we hear the most—even if those things are not true. So we need to be very aware about what we are allowing ourselves to hear. We need to get God's faith in us, so that if a time comes when we or someone we know needs healing, we have the faith to draw that power into our own personal reality.

Again, "Faith comes from hearing the message, and the message is heard through the Word of Christ."[3]

We don't know when we're going to need to draw from the reservoir of faith—of the power of possibility—for our lives. So we need to always be listening to the right sources, and be ready to put what we hear to action.

We gain faith in the things we hear the most.

My biggest faith challenge in the area of physical healing was when one of my sons was only 6 years old. He was diagnosed with tuberculosis (TB).

It all started with what we thought was just another ordinary check up before he started school, but there was nothing ordinary about this visit. The doctor said, after running various tests, that he had tested positive for TB.

As Missy and I stood there discussing what we had just been told, I began to have an inner dialog with myself: *Do I believe the Word of God? If I open my mouth and say that I receive this, then that is a giant my son will have to face every day for the rest of his life.*

Naturally speaking, there is no cure for TB. It can be controlled by taking a little pill every day, but it doesn't ever go away. Thoughts like, *It's just a little pill, quit worrying,* started racing through my mind.

Immediately I took those thoughts captive. *I DO believe the Word and the Word of God says that my son is healed by the stripes of Jesus!*

We don't know when we're going to need to draw from the reservoir of faith—of the power of possibility—for our lives. So we need to always be listening to the right sources, and be ready to put what we hear to action.

No, I wasn't going to stand for it. I knew that if I succumbed to the pressure of this giant, that a new giant would be waiting right around the next corner for my family. We weren't going to let that happen.

We got him some temporary medication and went home.

Immediately, I went to my prayer room and office, what I called the "upper room" over our garage, and I started talking to God about the situation. About an hour and half later, I was sure of the decision that there was no way we were going to receive the diagnosis of tuberculosis. We just wouldn't do it.

Please notice what I did not do. I didn't say, "Well, the doctor said it, so we believe him. We'll just have our son take the medication and he will learn to live with it." That would be reasonable, but no!

I also didn't call up that doctor, call him names, tell him what I thought about his diagnosis, and that we didn't receive it in the Name of Jesus. That kind of behavior does more harm than good. The doctor was doing his job. He was just calling it like he saw it— but that doctor didn't see the healing that was waiting in the realm of true power.

Instead, I did the responsible thing and gave our son his daily medication as per the doctor's orders—and I took the fight where it belonged.

"For our struggle is not against flesh and blood, but against the rulers, against the authorities, against the powers of this dark world and against the spiritual forces of evil in the heavenly realms."[4]

I began fasting. I fasted certain times that I normally spent watching TV. I fasted eating some foods I really enjoyed, and I began giving and sowing financial seed (money) into ministries that believed in healing.

Now let me take a side step here and address the practice of fasting. Fasting is to change you, not God. It is sacrificing something that costs you. For instance, if you don't like broccoli, then don't fast broccoli—that doesn't cost you anything. Fast from chocolate cake or cheeseburgers—something you really like.

And when you go to sow for healing—make sure it is into a ministry that believes in supernatural healing. If you are sowing for financial increase and breakthrough, then sow into a ministry that believes in supernatural financial breakthrough. You want to sow into good ground so your seed will produce fruit. We were believing for healing, so we sure weren't going to sow seed into a ministry that didn't believe in healing.

Genesis explains this principle of sowing and how it exists:

"While the earth remains, seedtime and harvest, cold and heat, winter and summer, and day and night shall not cease."[5] This principle works whether we are working it on purpose or not. We do reap what we sow—and we are always sowing whether we know it or not.

What God wants us to do, when we sow a seed, is sow it for a specific purpose. In other words, what is the intention of the seed you're sowing? Name it. God gets it! After all, He was the one who created this seedtime and harvest time system. Throughout the years of my life, I have sown seed for...

- Promotion...
- My future...
- My dreams...
- Protection and safety....

The list is endless and so are the results.

Now, fasting and sowing are not us trying to pay off God, or to get Him to feel sorry for us so He will give us a miracle. No, we can't do that. You can't buy off God! But what you can do is sow a seed into healing and reap a harvest of healing. He is moved by our faith. It pleases Him.[6]

OK, back to my story. I was doing everything I knew to do including declaring the Word, praising God and believing God. I laid hands on my son and I told him that he was healed. Of course, the neat thing about kids is that they believe everything their daddy says, so he believed for his own healing along with us.

Weeks went by and my flesh wanted to give up. I wanted an escape—even a brownie would do. The pressure of the battle raged on, but I didn't give in. I kept declaring. I kept praising. I kept right on doing what I knew to do.

I never will forget the night God woke me up about midnight. He said, "Your son is healed. Take him to the doctor."

Missy scheduled an appointment right away. They tested him again, and sure enough, no TB. We had them test him again—no TB. We had them run it one more time—no TB. He was healed.

We killed that giant because we didn't want that beast to be passed along to someone else in our lineage, to those who by heritage are waiting in our future.

Another thing I want to point out that's important for you to know and learn—through it all, my son was never in any pain. If he had been, I would have given him pain medication. Never exercise

---

"But without faith it is impossible to please and be satisfactory to Him. For whoever would come near to God must necessarily believe that God exists and that He is the rewarder of those who earnestly and diligently seek Him out."

Hebrews 11:6

---

your faith on your kids while you're developing it. Exercise your faith on yourself first. If you can't get your own headache healed, then don't think you can get your kid healed of TB or any other disease. Get your faith built up so if the time ever arises that a giant tries to take ground in your world, you can slay him and go on.

You may not have any issues today. Everything may be going according to plan. Praise God. But it's always important to live by faith, to strengthen your faith every day, to train yourself while times are good, instead of readying yourself in the heat of the battle!

This parallel universe where the power of possibility exists—the eternal realm—can only be accessed by faith, because faith and belief honor the unseen reality where heaven's power is resident. Therefore, you must build your faith so when you need the power of possibility, you can receive it easily and quickly.

God, through Jesus Christ, has given us great freedoms, and 2,000 years later, Jesus is still setting the captive free, with the freedoms that are resident inside Him. The freedom on the inside of Jesus is so great, it's more than enough to liberate every person in every generation for all time. And once we're free, our freedom is no longer His responsibility. It's mine. It's yours. It's ours. So, the responsibility for your life, your marriage, family, body, and money is on you.

One day the Holy Spirit said to me, "Never, ever, ever turn your body over to anyone else. I'm holding you accountable for it."

Yes, doctors are valuable, but don't just take their word for it. People are misdiagnosed every day. He said, "Keep Me in the loop."

This parallel universe where healing, abundance, prosperity and blessing exist can only be accessed by faith because only belief honors the unseen reality.

He was referring to His leadership of my life. The Bible tells us that our bodies are the temples of the Holy Ghost, so what He was telling me made sense.[7]

He also said, "Your body is first yours, then my responsibility. It's ours together—yours and the Holy Spirit's. It's nurtured and resourced through your relationship with Me. The same spirit that raised Christ from the dead dwells in you and He will quicken your mortal body.[8] I will see to it, with your relational pursuit of Me that your health is renewed, recovery is quick, and that you live full of strength and vitality."

The Holy Spirit again said, "Never give the responsibilities of your freedom to someone else. The healing initiative of your life, body and money is on you. Never turn the responsibility of your money over to anyone else."

Money professionals—financial planners and bankers—are getting rich off others. Many are making fortunes off other people who simply won't take the initiative or responsibility for their life experience. Make a commitment to be responsible for your freedom. Become responsible to the Holy Spirit for your life, health, marriage, relationships and money."

God is so good to us! He is for us! He wants us to experience the power of possibility in every area of our lives.

I immediately thought of the verse that says, "Beloved, I pray that you may prosper in all things and be in health, just as your soul prospers."[9]

The things God speaks to us will never contradict His Word. He is faithful to His Word.

The Holy Spirit went on to say to me, "I can't give you everything. I can only give you my part. My desire is for your spiritual, physical, emotional, relational and financial health and prosperity."

God is so good to us! He is for us! He wants us to experience the power of possibility in every area of our lives. And He wanted my son to experience it for sure!

WILL YOU WALK IN FAITH OR UNBELIEF?

For my son to be healed, we had to stay in a place of faith in our hearts and minds. We had to stay in a place of agreement about his healing. We couldn't afford to let in any unbelief. The consequences would have led to our destruction—to his never being healed.

Unbelief—or doubt—will erode your confidence in God's Word and what you're expecting the power of possibility to change in your life. Unbelief will always get you what you expect. Unbelief is actually faith in something other than God. Its implication is that your "seen reality" is superior to the "unseen reality," but that is never true. Faith is founded on the "unseen reality" being superior to any circumstance or situation that we face in the seen world.

As believers, we must remember that our understanding is framed by faith. The Bible says by faith we understand, or we could say it this way, we understand by faith.[10]

So, as a believer, faith should be the foundation for all of our intellectualism. We have to learn by faith and understand by faith. When we do that, we grow our faith and trust in God, and we come

---

It didn't make sense when Peter walked on water, but by faith he did.

---

to understand that faith doesn't require our natural understanding—acquired through the accumulation of facts and knowledge—to function. To rely on our natural understanding would be to repeat Adam and Eve's mistake. They obeyed the deceitful voice of mankind's adversary (Satan) and their five physical senses confirmed what their adversary was saying. They relied on their natural understanding vs. mixing in their faith, too. In other words—it may seem impossible, it may not even make sense, but God said it, and what He said makes faith.

It didn't make sense that my son was healed when he had tested positive for an incurable disease, but by faith, he was, and it became our reality and still is 15 years later.

It didn't make sense when Peter walked on water, but by faith he did.

Faith knows beyond all doubt that spiritual reality is superior and God desires for us to live from that reality—in total health, prosperity, abundance and peace. It is from that reality that we access the power of possibility.

But to live in that place of faith, we have to quit trying to understand God with our limited thinking. We must understand by faith. This allows us to move into a deeper relationship with Him by trusting Him. That's when faith becomes easy. In fact, we have to trust Him with a blind faith—like a child trusts Mom and Dad. Isn't it interesting that it says, "We walk by faith, not by sight"? Faith doesn't require sight. It doesn't require the "seen reality" to confirm the "unseen world."

Faith knows beyond all doubt that spiritual reality is superior and God desires for us to live from that reality—in total health, prosperity, abundance and peace. It is from that reality that we access the power of possibility.

Jesus told us that we must have the faith of a child or we cannot enter the kingdom of Heaven.[11] Children are born trusting. They trust their parents to feed, bathe and clothe them. They have to— they can't do it themselves. And they continue to trust unless they are taught not to. It's only when their trust is broken that they begin to doubt.

That is the kind of trust we are to have in our Heavenly Father—a complete faith because He has never done anything to break that trust.

Now the devil fights us for power—for our faith. That's why there is such a hostile attack on our relationship with God. Our enemy knows that when things that seem impossible to overcome are overtaken by the power of possibility, trust and faith are restored between men and God. He knows where our healing, prosperity and peace is, and he will do whatever he can to stop us from possessing it. He wants distance between God and us. So, we must guard our source of power—faith—so it can produce the results we need.

Since faith comes by hearing, one of the first ways the devil will try to get at your faith is through what you are hearing. He will put people around you, sometimes your closest friends and family, who will contradict God's existence and God's Word.

The truth is, we love these people. They are our family, but if they are speaking things contrary to the Word of God about our circumstances, then we may have to limit the value we place on their advice, without offending them of course.

In reality, our faith is growing in something, or someone today. That could be the voice of the evening news—CNN or CNBC. It could be Aunt Sally or Uncle Henry. It could be your college professor, your favorite philosopher, your physician, or your money manager. If you value any one voice above God's voice, your faith will be

All of God's strategies are designed to make faith.

built in them instead of God. Left unattended, faith will turn into doubt and unbelief. And as much as you may admire a particular person, they possess no power to radically alter your circumstances supernaturally. They possess no powers of possibility.

When my son was sick, do you think I listened to the people who said the disease wasn't curable? No, I didn't even receive what the doctor said. By that I mean that I respected him and his diagnosis, but I didn't receive it as the final word. I didn't take it into my heart. I didn't believe it. But if I had called up the doctor every day and talked about the hopelessness of a cure, then I would have begun to believe in that instead of the reality he could be healed.

You have to guard your faith by putting a guard on your ears. Faith comes by hearing, and so does doubt and unbelief. Make sure you are listening to the Word of God and building faith in the supernatural dimension. That's where the power lies!

All of God's strategies are designed to make faith. They are the doors of your success.

CHAPTER 3

CLEAR OUT
RELATIONAL HOSTILITY

BEFORE IT STEALS YOUR FAITH

One thing we must know is that the enemy is always trying to steal our faith. He knows its power to propel our lives into our destiny—and he'll steal it anyway he can. He robs us of our faith primarily in two ways: by creating distance between us and God, and creating distance—or division—between us and other people. I call it relational hostility. Genuine Christianity is designed to unite us, but relational hostility is designed to separate us.

As a country, we have seen religious leaders fall into adultery and political figures thrown into jail for countless acts of lawlessness. We have seen parents and teachers abuse children, and been the victim of abuse ourselves. The devil uses these circumstances to entice us to think that there is not anyone who can ever be trusted.

Jesus said, "In the last days many offenses will come."[1] The purpose for those offenses is to bring you into captivity, rob you of your freedom, and bring people into bondage once again.

During a time when Missy and I were being tested relationally, the Holy Spirit said, "The wall between you and that person can

37

become the ceiling between you and God. Keep that wall down and you'll live under open heavens."

More than money challenges, physical symptoms or career problems, relational hostility can erode our faith. So we have to live in a place of continual forgiveness and extending unconditional love.

Jesus said there are only two commands—not 22 million—just love God and love people.[2] I've simplified it, because it really is elementary. Our relationship with people reveals our relationship with

---

Genuine Christianity is designed to unite us.

God. So when Jesus said, "And if he sins against you seven times in a day, and seven times in a day returns to you, saying, 'I repent,' you shall forgive him." Later the disciples responded with, "Lord, increase our faith."[3]

Over the years, Missy and I have met with many individuals who have had situations in their lives where they needed help—and many times it was concerning relational hostility. We have listened as they have told us, detail by detail, about how someone hurt them—which is really "code talk" for being offended. Missy has often asked, "When did all this happen?" (Thinking it was in the past few weeks).

Their response is usually something like 15 or 20 years ago. But even if it was just one to five years ago, they remain paralyzed by an event that still controls their decisions and actions with disastrous consequences.

I have found that people will completely and utterly dismiss what God says about that relational issue just to hold on to their hurt. It seems as though their hurt has become a sort of comfort zone, and they truly believe God's all right with it!

As pastors, we often talk people off the ledge who are dealing with emotions from an event that happened years ago. Despite the freedom of forgiveness and the gospel we preach, people continue living in their negative past to their own detriment.

God wants you free from the hurt of relational hostility. We all get hurt from time to time, but we can't live holding on to that hurt. I can remember one time in a church service having everyone raise their hand if they had ever been hurt by anyone. Every hand went up in the place! So its obvious we may have been hurt, but the odds are we've probably hurt others, too. We all have to forgive and let go, or we put ourselves in an emotional prison. Set yourself free! Forgive!

This is the picture the Lord gave me to help me overcome: When I was 9 years old, my dad started a new career. We sold the house and moved. Years later, we'd go by the old neighborhood. I'd say to myself, *We lived there.* But I had no attraction to that thing in my

---

God wants you free from the hurt of relational hostility. We all get hurt from time to time, but we can't live holding on to that hurt.

---

past. Since you have no attraction to that thing, don't go back! The real point is that if you are living captive by your past, then the very person who hurt you is manipulating you. They are controlling your emotions and influencing your decisions and perspectives. And believe me, they have moved on, and so should you.

During our relational journeys we've come to understand that when we become more sensitive to people we become insensitive to God. In other words, the order of Jesus' command is to love God, then love people. It's not to love people, then to love God. But hurt feelings can cause us to put this person we dislike first, in front of God, in a negative way. Do you see the perspective?

Missy said this once about relational hostility as we were taping our TV show: "If you don't take it personally, you won't take it." It's so true. You can desensitize yourself to negative people—and your past—by building your faith in your relationship with God. Put your trust in His love for you. When you put your trust in Him, you begin to recognize He didn't hurt you—an imperfect person did.

There have been times as pastors where we have just had to say in the most loving way, "Ok, we've prayed over that. We've prayed the prayer of forgiveness. We've bound it up, we've cast it out, and we've loosed it. Together, we've thrown it into the sea of forgetfulness. We are not going back there with you."

Surprisingly, there were times this brought relational separation between us and the people we were helping. People acted as if they couldn't possibly forgive, and deflected the problem on us—the two

---

It takes great faith to forgive those who have offended you.

---

people who were simply in the role of "Life Coach." Their hurt became so much a part of their comfort—of their identity—that they couldn't turn loose of it even though Jesus says if you won't forgive your brother, I won't forgive you.[4]

It takes great faith to forgive those who have offended you, betrayed you, slandered you or abused you. It takes great faith to forgive people whose desire is for you to fail, to forgive those who seemingly work tirelessly against you. This is why love is necessary. "Love never fails."[5]

Love is unconditional—it is the one characteristic in your life as a believer that ultimately defines your level of spiritual maturity. Love empowers you to let people go so their transgression doesn't get lodged in your soul. In turn, your faith continues to work effortlessly without muddling through negative emotions and double-mindedness. Don't let offense get between you and your God, or allow unforgiveness to deactivate your faith. Not only does unforgiveness keep you from trusting people, but also it ultimately affects your faith in God.

Love is unconditional.

Offense and unforgiveness are lies, and the lies of our enemy—the devil—are like poison that contaminates our hearts and changes our ability to transfer our trust and faith from this "seen reality" to the "unseen reality."

Recently, when we were traveling, Missy and I read an article that reported more than 12,000 laptops are left in airports every week. Not every year—every week! Most of them are left at the security checkpoints—by accident—and 70 percent of the people don't ever go back and recover them!

I find this so surprising, but we can do the same thing in life. We can be in such a hurry—moving on to the next thing, the next relationship, the next city, the next spouse, the next job, because we are hurt, and that pain is affecting our actions and our choices to such a degree—that we never stop and ask, "What happened there? What was that all about? What was I supposed to take from that experience to resource my life later? What does God say about this?" Sometimes these are hard questions to ask, but we must move forward, and asking those questions is part of moving forward in a healthy way.

If we become like the person rushing through security at the airport with valuable data, we will miss taking what is rightfully ours that we need to grow.

As a voice of value, I'm asking you to hit the pause button of your life. I know the season of life you're in may be rough, and you may feel like your life is falling apart. If so, my first question is, "What's been holding it together?"

If it's not God, that's why it's falling apart around you.

You need to commit to God, and start with asking Him for forgiveness. Then you can pursue Him relationally with your whole being. He will catch you before you hit the ground, even though religion will tell you to clean up first. God doesn't care about where

---

Get to know God and make Him your Father.

---

you've been, or what you have or haven't done. He cares about you in your present. If your statement is, "My life is falling apart," and you have a relationship with God, then you simply need to build your faith in Him, not just in what you have heard about Him. Paul said, "For I know in whom I have believed."[6] It's not what you know—it's whom you know.

MERCY TRIUMPHS OVER JUDGMENT—EVERY TIME

If you believe your life is in a meltdown, then you need to know Him, His character, His wisdom, and His mercy better. God is not one-dimensional, leaning heavily toward judgment. The Bible doesn't say, "God's judgments are new every morning." Wrong! It says His mercies are new every morning.[7] In fact, it also says that mercy triumphs over judgment—every time![8] It goes on to say judgment without mercy will be shown to anyone who has not been merciful.

God said He would uphold you with the right hand—a symbol of His power—of His righteousness. Get to know God and make Him your Father. He will keep you, even if your life has been shattered into millions of broken pieces. Many times it's only God who can put Humpty Dumpty back together again. So whether He catches you before you fall, or while your life is falling apart, even if your life is in pieces today, when God gets through with you, not only will you be whole, but also your life will be positioned for significance.

He is so faithful to us that He promises: "If any of you lacks wisdom, he should ask God, who gives generously to all without finding fault, and it will be given to him."[9]

Do you recognize God's approach to your life? How He sees you? He's not a faultfinder like people who are so transfixed on our previous mistakes. People don't forget, but God will. Hey, God's over it already. Generously forgive yourself and forget your past failures so that you can delight in life.

God is not one-dimensional, leaning heavily toward judgment. God's mercies are new every morning—not His judgments.

Practice directing action toward your loves instead of living from your hates, and don't continue to allow your hurt to motivate you in the wrong direction. Work at not allowing yourself to be so sensitive to people—what they say, what they do, what they think. That kind of hyper-sensitivity will make their acceptance or rejection of you become greater than God's acceptance of you.

Remember, when you do allow them to hurt you, the pain gets stuck in your inner world. If the hurt is lodged in you, regardless of the distance between you and them, it's still in you—and it will affect your life, and despite what you may think, you can't make hurt go away through separation from that person, because your feelings of hurt are only a response to what is in your inner life. That's why hurting people hurt other people. If you want your life to be comparatively different this year than from last year, then live intentionally. Forgive for your sake! Then you can be released from their grip. That kind of intentional living will alter the course of your life drastically.

Missy and I have built into our relationships less and less tolerance for the kind of behavior that repeats foolishness. You know, the kind where we go another round of judgment, offense, strife and unforgiveness. We have less tolerance of believers we're close to acting as if this is the first time they've heard to walk in love and forgive. I'm talking about longtime believers—people who know better, but have the gall to act as if it's an unknown. So we have built into

---

If you want your life to be comparatively different this year than from last year, then live intentionally. Forgive for your sake!

---

our relationships a "covenant accountability" that says, "I can't be a part of fixing what's broken in your life, because you keep breaking yourself. You keep repeating that volunteer cycle over and over again—the kind of behavior where you volunteer by default, by not living intentionally."

When you make a decision to not buy into the devil's tactics, you become more aware and guard your faith even more closely. Your faith is a precious asset and the key to unlocking a whole new world where everything that seems impossible is altered drastically for your good. With God the possibilities are endless and His faith was designed so you can succeed in everyday life.

He wants you to learn to use it NOW for every situation. If you learn to use it now, then it can pave the way for a better tomorrow.

CHAPTER 4

MIX FAITH & WISDOM NOW

LEARN HOW TO BE A "TODAY'S BELIEVER" TO PRODUCE A BETTER TOMORROW

I'm a bit of a history buff, especially church history. So, through the years, I've tracked what God was doing and where. Even as a child, my mom spoke frequently to me about "the moves of God." Back then she was referring to the miracle revivals of the 50s, the healing revivals of the 60s, and the Jesus Movement of the 70s—the one that began outside of the four walls of the church among long-haired hippies, who weren't welcome in denominational churches. I realized much later she was bragging on God—talking Him up! She was honoring what God had done—how He had moved—in the earth!

Because of her influence and value on what God had done, as I grew older, I kept an eye on how God was moving in my generation—nationally and globally. I noticed that in the 70s, there was an overlap of how God was restoring healing and a new move of the Holy Spirit. It was labeled the Charismatic Movement and was characterized by mainstream denominations accepting the ministry and manifestations of the Holy Spirit. Traditionally conservative denominations were embracing an undeniable revolution of the person of the Holy Spirit. The result was a freedom in worship and expression. In the 80s, all these movements continue to exist, and the message of faith was introduced. The understanding of using our faith to move mountains and please God in a purposeful way was revolutionary. The message that accompanied this, that God was a good God, was freedom to generations who had lived thinking of God as far away, impersonal and demanding. We began to realize that if it's good, it's God!

Despite the revelation and immense value of each move, I noticed that initially only a remnant of people embraced each one, but then slowly that acceptance began to get traction and spread.

In the 80s and early 90s, the prosperity message spread and met strong resistance. This was the message that, according to covenant, God wants His people blessed. He wants us living blessed lives. It is

God is bringing the heavenly forces of faith and wisdom to produce a combinational force that is undeniable, unstoppable, even unbreakable.

built on the revelation of the goodness of God. Today, this revelation, too, is a dominant belief in mainstream denominations. Certainly, there have been misuses, but most people understand the truth of the message and embrace it, even if they call it by another name. Regardless of what you call it—being blessed or being prosperous—the Word says God wants us to prosper in our spirits, souls and bodies. He cares about our whole being.

As I witnessed and experienced each of these moves of God, I recognized how each one built on the other. I experienced the excitement and expectation of the supernatural building of each move combining with the next move. I lived in the momentum of revelation and growth that grew through the moves. It was amazing.

I remember people gathering for lunch or dinner and speaking about what God was doing. They were excited as they shared about the revelation they received. They recognized the tangible power of His presence embedded in the message and couldn't wait to talk about it.

What were they doing? Talking God up! Bragging on Him!

They spoke with great joy of what was happening. They lived the scripture saying, "This is the Lord's doing. It's marvelous in our eyes."[1] They were actually praising and worshipping God by talking

> *It's time to talk up God. It's time to talk up*
> *His goodness.*

Him up. They were saying something good about God. God loves that! He loves it so much, He comes and inhabits the praises of His people.[2] He comes into our midst when we praise Him!

Today, now that we are more than a decade into the new millennium, God is bringing the heavenly forces of faith and wisdom to produce a combinational force that is undeniable, unstoppable, even unbreakable. So it's time to start talking again. It's time to talk up God. It's time to talk up His goodness. Those of us who have received the truth of each move over the last 60 years are living with a strength no other generation of believers has ever possessed. We are a generation of believers who have the power to live in today—and it affect our tomorrow powerfully. We don't have to be looking ahead to moves of God—even though more moves may come. Our "tomorrow" is "here today!" We don't have to be looking to the horizon for what's next to experience all God's called us to accomplish. We have tremendous power available now!

As I said, I watched the moves of God. My parents made me aware of them by pointing them out to me: "Scott, look at what

God did in this decade and then in that decade. Look at what He's doing now."

Not only did this build a filter through which I viewed the world, the church, and the believer, but also it showed me what God was successfully doing: building progression of restoration into a life of

---

God wants us living continually in the unforced rhythms of grace.

---

abundance intended for every believer.[3] God's progression of restoration is designed to salvage and reclaim the Christian's life that has been postponed, misplaced, stolen or lost because of their preoccupation with other things. It is evidence of His mercy and love!

Not only was I seeing, hearing and experiencing this, but also I was learning the rhythms of heaven. I was seeing what God had wanted from the beginning—and it was clear, He would not let it be delayed ever again.

LEARNING TO LIVE IN THE UNFORCED RHYTHMS OF GRACE

While the moves of God were great—and they got us to where we are today—they aren't the way God wants us to live. The moves were important. Each one progressed the Body of Christ into a greater understanding of God's goodness and the manifestation of His grace. But He doesn't want us living from event to event, or move to move. He wants us living continually in the unforced rhythms of grace.

I like how one version speaks to us so clearly: "Are you tired? Worn out? Burned out on religion? Come to me. Get away with me and you'll recover your life. I'll show you how to take a real rest. Walk with me and work with me—watch how I do it. Learn the unforced rhythms of grace. I won't lay anything heavy or ill fitting on you. Keep company with me and you'll learn to live freely and lightly."[4]

You and I are not predisposed to grace. We are not hard-wired to live this way. Our DNA is missing the "grace gene." We like things forced, structured, black and white, clear-cut, and lawful. Our human nature makes us think we must work for it. We must qualify through a series of holy activities to earn our place with God. Only then do we think we deserve heavenly benefits. When someone's experience with God is forced, it's not God—it's actually religion. Jesus said we must learn the unforced rhythms of grace. We must

---

You and I are not predisposed to grace. Our human nature makes us think we must work for it.

---

learn to walk with Him, and work with Him. It's like taking a real rest, learning to live freely and lightly.

Instead of worrying about our performance, we should focus on God's acceptance of us. Religion wears us out, wears us down, and removes the joy that exists in a relationship with Him.

What does your experience with God look like? Is it a struggle? Is it hard without emotional encounters with Him? Is it burdensome? Has it grown more distant and less frequent?

If you said, "Yes," to any of these, then learn the unforced rhythms of grace. It's in this rhythm that your experience with God, Jesus and the Holy Spirit—three distinct individuals with three completely different approaches to your life—will lead you out of the world of fantasy and unreality into a whole new reality with Him.

Jesus was talking about this rhythm of grace when He said, "Take my yoke upon you and learn from me, for I am gentle and humble in heart, and you will find rest for your souls. For My yoke is easy and My burden is light."[5] He wants us to "yoke up together with Him."

Jesus talked about yokes, because in His day, a farmer yoked a young ox with an older ox to teach the young one strength and stamina, and to become more powerful and mature. The reason for a "yoked relationship" with Jesus is to learn how to walk in step and work in step with Him—to become more powerful and more ma-

> *For every challenge you're facing, you have a measure of faith from God, designated to that specific trouble.*

ture. According to the Word, the world is anxiously anticipating this event: "All of creation is waiting for the mature sons of God."[6]

This is a call into partnership with God, where we learn the unforced rhythms of grace individually, while simultaneously becoming corporately mobilized.

The new believer is here today, and we will manifest on the earth in our generation, living in an unforced rhythm that is fueled by grace.

So as we learn, we no longer live as yesterday's believer. We aren't looking to moves, or living from move to move. We no longer live around the triumphs of the believer of the past, but we are the believer of today, because faith is now. It's not in our past. It's not in our future. It's in our present.[7]

LIVE AS A TODAY'S BELIEVER

For every challenge you're facing, you have a measure of faith from God, designated to that specific trouble. "God has dealt to every man the measure of faith."[8]

Therefore, let's hypothetically say someone is dealing with financial odds stacked against them—mortgage debt, car payments, student loans, credit cards that are maxed out. They got themselves in a financial hole, because after all, God didn't spend the money.

Well, the first law of holes is stop digging. Back away from the credit card. (LOL) Cut it up or freeze it in a bowl of water where you can't use it because of a spur of the moment decision. Then get to work on a solution.

Here's the truth. God has given you a measure of faith to not only put the brakes on a problem, but also to solve it.

Years ago, Missy and I, in our immaturity, were living in such debt. Even though we were Christians, and knew all the teachings on finances, our credit card debts alone were more than $40,000. For a couple of kids in their mid 30s with a few kids of their own, it was overwhelming.

We sat down at our desk where we conducted family business, and calculated and crunched the numbers until we had a real understanding of just what kind of hole we had dug for ourselves—

We all must become responsible for our own personal freedom that Christ gave us and appropriate it correctly.

---

one we'd dug all by our lonesome without any of God's help. We didn't cry and say, "God, why did you do this to us?" or "Why did you allow this?"

No, we came to the conclusion that it was our responsibility. We did this to ourselves. God gave us the freedom, but He didn't use our freedom for us. That's why each one of us must become responsible for our own personal freedom that Christ gave us and appropriate it correctly. If we don't manage it properly, our freedom will create an opportunity for the flesh, and our flesh's appetite is never satisfied.

Missy and I had to build an emotion toward our debt. We built hatred toward debt, and it felt as real as the emotion of embarrassment or the feeling of an illness. We wanted to feel it and absorb it so we weren't numb to it. We didn't want to feel like we were in denial of it—which we weren't. We compared it to the feelings of sickness.

In this process, we also repented, asked God for forgiveness for living presumptuously, and asked God for a plan to get out of the financial mess we were in.

Not long after that on a sunny Sunday afternoon after church and lunch with family, I took a notebook and pen and went to the dining room. I said to the Lord, "OK, Lord, show me."

> *The power of possibility's potential is so vast it can absorb all the evidence of poverty, lack or debt in your life.*

He said, "Start with My Word." I began to write out scriptures that dealt with my money problem, and at some point I continued past writing scriptures into writing a plan.

Several hours later, we had it: "Heaven's strategy." It was a plan for debt elimination. In it were several things God told us to do that didn't make sense, like increase our giving—but they made faith.

Missy and I took communion over the plan and settled our decision to commit to it in our hearts. Nothing happened overnight, but that didn't matter. In executing this strategy, we figured it would take 5-6 years to get completely free. However, what we didn't figure was the power of possibility encapsulated in the strategy itself. Supernaturally, we were out of credit card debt in 18 months, and out of car debt in 32 months.

You see, God had dealt a measure of faith specifically for that area of our lives that was more powerful than the debt itself. And God has made the same power available to you.

Friend, you are more valuable, more precious than any amount of money. Just like money doesn't define you, neither does your debt. It's not who you are. Our debt wasn't who we were. It was just a mess we'd gotten ourselves into.

So do not get under the sting of condemnation and guilt regarding whatever mess you might be in. The power of possibility's potential is so vast it can absorb all the evidence of poverty, lack or debt in

---

Just like there is no substitute for faith, there is equally no substitute for heaven's wisdom.

---

your life. Like a sponge, it will soak up every ounce of "not enough's" residue until it is completely absorbed. Then, all that will be left in its place is abundance, plenteousness and increase. God didn't just give us the measure of faith, He also gave us a wisdom (a plan) and the faith to go with it. Then, as we executed the wisdom in faith, He added the power of possibility to it. He added His supernatural power on our natural power.

Just like there is no substitute for faith, there is equally no substitute for heaven's wisdom, even though religion has created two different camps—the faith camp and the wisdom camp. In many cases it seems like the faith camp has kissed their brains goodbye—not doing what's naturally smart and then needing one miracle moment after the next—while the wisdom camp, by their own admission, are the "realists" who seem void of an ounce of faith. God never intended for either of these to live without the other. We're to live by faith, in the wisdom of God!

As today's believer, who has grown up in the fruit of all these moves of God, we are the generation that will bring both of these substances—faith and wisdom—together. Both of these substances are heavenly:

• "Now faith is confidence in what we hope for and assurance about what we do not see."[9]

• "The beginning of wisdom is this: Get wisdom. Though it cost all you have, get understanding."[10]

God gave wisdom and faith to us so we could create a more powerful substance by mixing them together. Faith connected to wisdom's strategy is an unstoppable power that transcends anything we confront—even those situations that seem impossible.

Let me explain: When I was a younger man, I drank "Dr. Peppers®." It's known as the cola of Texas. Now, I didn't drink Dr. Peppers® in moderation, like one or two a day. I drank six, seven or eight

---

God gave wisdom and faith to us so we could create a more powerful substance by mixing them together.

---

a day—and too much of a good thing is never good! During this season of my life, I was having various symptoms in my body. And as much as I tried, I could not figure them out.

I took the time to read the Bible and find scriptures to pray and stand on in faith concerning these specific physical problems. I knew God's promises to me as a believer for health and healing. I locked on to the scriptures that dealt with my issues, and intentionally began to obtain my inheritance of healing, but absolutely nothing changed. In fact, my symptoms grew worse, much worse. One of the symptoms was sores in my mouth that were very painful. Another was abdominal swelling and pain. But no matter the pain, I stayed the course spiritually in what seemed like a never-ending struggle. Each week ran into the next with no changes.

Then one day, as I was at work in my office taking a break, having a Dr. Pepper® over ice, I heard that still small voice inside me say, "Your problem is what you're drinking." It was the Holy Spirit directing me. I took another drink and said to myself, *"No way, that couldn't be it."*

At this point, the voice in my spirit had my attention because I had heard that voice many times before. It wasn't my voice or even my inner voice. I had learned in my relationship with God how to distinguish between my mind—my inner voice—and His voice. (This is another subject entirely, but since my Dr. Pepper® days, I

Wisdom and faith produce such peace—such healing and emotional wholeness—when we allow them to work together in our lives.

---

also have learned the value of distinguishing the voices of which person of the trinity is directing me—God my father, Jesus my brother or the Holy Spirit my counselor. They are three unique individuals with three specific relational approaches to my life—and yours. Yes, I'm saying you can know specifically which person of the Godhead is speaking to you.)

So I said, "Holy Spirit, speak to me about this." And His counsel, like that of a skilled physician who knows the intricate workings of the body, detailed my painful experience to me. The wisdom of God, like a lightning bolt flashed through me. I knew that was it. The Holy Spirit was spot on!

I didn't take another sip of Dr. Pepper® for two years after that. Immediately, because I made the choice to follow the wisdom the Holy Spirit was speaking to me, and follow it in faith, I began to feel better. The next day all of my symptoms were completely gone as if they never existed.

Do you see the process of what happened? The heavenly substance of wisdom invaded my mind, accompanied by the heavenly substance of faith. This combinational force, in the midst of what seemed like an impossible situation to me, released the power of possibility into my body and brought simple resolution.

Wisdom and faith produce such peace—such healing and emotional wholeness—when we allow them to work together in our lives. "God has dealt to every man the measure of faith."[11]

The Bible isn't a book filled with mere words, it's an invitation to understand God's world. Notice what matters to God in the following verses:

"My people perish for a lack of **knowledge**."[12]

"And with all thy getting, get **understanding**."[13]

"**Wisdom** is the principal thing."[14]

We are to elevate all the way into the heights of God's wisdom. Jesus didn't just grow in knowledge or even understanding. Jesus grew in wisdom.

There are three levels revealed in these words. Each one possesses a certain degree of power. The first is knowledge. As the old saying goes, "Knowledge is power." Like Adam and Eve, the world is in pursuit of the knowledge of good and evil, however, God's guidance suggests that we reach far beyond the shallowness of just knowledge. We need to move on into the dimension of understanding. We are to elevate all the way into the heights of God's wisdom. Jesus didn't just grow in knowledge or even understanding. Jesus grew in wisdom.[15] Wisdom was His primary focus. It is the understanding of God's world, ways, perspectives and realities—and when applied to our lives, it brings about optimum results, the outcome that supersedes the norm.

Now, let's apply all of this to your life. Perhaps you are spiraling out of control from financial pressure. Maybe you are weighted down by what seems like insurmountable debt. Yes, it seems impossible that you could ever pay it all off, but God has given you a measure of His faith for that.

Or, maybe you are experiencing relational hostility from someone who is a close friend or ally. Relational betrayal and conflict is

---

God's is for you—on your side with you—and not against you.

---

one of the most stressful situations your soul will encounter, and it creates great pain accompanied by personal feelings of rejection. It can devastate your inner world and erode your confidence. But God has given you the measure of faith for that as well.

Whatever your challenge, it can be complicated by sickness, ailments or potential bouts of depression—which are all common side effects of a test or trial—but even so, God also has given you the measure of faith to counter that.

Yes, sometimes when it rains, it pours, and God has given us the measure of faith to counter it all. When trials come at us all at once, what seems impossible is not because God has given you a counter-force to combat the trials. God will not allow you to be tested above what you're able to bear.[16]

I know at times it seems like He does, but be assured, God will not allow that. With every seemingly impossible situation, adding up like the proverbial straw that broke the camel's back, you need to realize, through Christ, you are becoming even stronger, more powerful, and more capable of overcoming—when you mix faith and wisdom to fight your battles.

The odds are stacked against you in this natural realm. But God's is for you—on your side with you—and not against you. He's given

---

God is planning for your life today. His plan is not what you learn to do—it's what you were born to do.

---

you the measure of faith. Now, look for the necessary wisdom to accompany it—God's strategy—and you will release the power of possibility into your life. That's living as a today's believer!

GOD'S PLAN FOR YOUR LIFE

Know this: God has a specific plan for you. The Prophet Jeremiah told us God's promise: "'For I know the plans I have for you,' declares the Lord, 'plans to prosper you and not to harm you, plans to give you hope and a future.'"[17]

So the question that begs asking is: "Do you not only trust God, but also, do you trust His plan for your life?"

God is planning for your life today. He's not just thinking and "day dreaming" about you. And His plan is not what you learn to do—it's what you were born to do. The things you learn in life only contribute to the fulfillment of His plan. When thinking about God's plan and purpose for my life, what resonates constantly throughout the corridors of my mind is Mom's voice: "Scott, as a 4-5-year-old boy, you would go to the street corner and preach every day."

My understanding of what she was telling me was this: "Cats meow, ducks quack and preachers preach." In other words, like me, you were hard-wired for something specific, a bent to which you are predisposed—and we all are. Your joy is discovered when you find God's plan for your life and live in it. I thank God every day for my assignment to be a preacher, and my motivation to fulfill God's plan for my life.

God said through Jeremiah, "If it's not good, it's not God's plan." His plan is not to hurt you or harm you, and His plan doesn't include failure, disease or financial destruction. In fact, God says those things are not in His plan for your life. God's plan is to prosper you, and to give you hope. Believe it, God's plan is to give you a future.

Without a doubt, we all have dreams, but without a plan, your dreams will never become a reality. So plan your life within the boundaries of prosperity, hope and the future. Have a spiritual plan, a prayer plan, and a relational plan. Take the time to have a study plan. Attempt to have a plan for every season of your life and every area in every season. When you make sure your plans are targeting what you were born to do, your dreams will become reality!

I can hear you now: "Yes, I want to get to my dreams, but are my

---

We all have dreams, but without a plan, your dreams will never become a reality.

---

dreams God's dreams? I've been working my plan so long, I don't know if it's His or mine or a combination of the two. I don't even know where to begin."

Somewhere around my 40s, I began to realize, if I always get my way, how will I know whether it's my plan or God's plan? Maybe this is a question you could ask yourself. If you have an itch that you always scratch, and all you ever do in life is do it your way...when you want to do it, how you want to do it, and where you want to do it...then you'll never distinguish between God and yourself.

If you live self-indulgent, when God tells you to do something you don't want to do, then you won't! You'll say, "That couldn't be God." You will have worked disciplines out of your life—ones that you'll need to do what He asks.

To prevent this from happening to me, I've introduced disciplines into my life by doing things I don't want to do. The list is long but a few include running, working out, praying, studying, reading, fasting certain foods, memorizing scripture and other information—anything to get out of my comfort zone. I've built a lifestyle of doing things I don't want to do, so that when God tells me to do some-

God has given you graces to overwhelm the forces of impossibility.

thing I don't want to do, I do it anyway. I've come to realize His ways are not my ways. And humility admits it, becomes aware of it, and then embraces His ways. Over time, it actually makes His ways and plans my own!

I've learned to stay out of any comfort zone that would affect my relationship with God negatively. I have learned to not only trust God, but also to trust His plan for my life.

MIX FAITH AND WISDOM

Inside God's plan for your life is a force positioned to be released into action with the use of your faith. It is designed to assault all that has been aligned against you. It is a promise so big, it works against any odds: "No weapon formed against you will prosper.[18] According to the power in this verse, every weapon used against you will be shut down—made unusable—when you mix your faith and God's wisdoms.

God has given you graces to overwhelm the forces of impossibility. When you're dealing with challenges on multiple fronts, and God has given you a measure of faith for each and every challenge, then there's a lot more faith swirling around your life than normal. It is God's plan to jump off the pages of the Bible and into the pages of our lives. He does that through our experiences of faith and wisdom.

God is a believer, so He has no problem believing. He has no issues with expecting great things to happen. He believes in healing. He believes in prosperity. He believes in peace and wholeness. He believes in restoration and abundant, extravagant living. Since He has no problem with believing, neither should we since we're "in Him." This means we're a part of God. "For you died, and your life is hidden with Christ in God."[19]

Leave the problem of unbelief to the "unbelieving believers." Jesus did. He understood how the reasoning of the religious robbed them of a relational experience with God.

Keep yourself mentally and emotionally where you are spiritually—in Him. "If you abide in Me, and My words abide in you, you will ask what you desire, and it shall be done for you."[20]

David—a man after God's own heart, knew this all too well

God is a believer, so He has no problem believing. He has no issues with expecting great things to happen. Since He has no problem with believing, neither should we.

---

when he declared, "He who dwells in the secret place of the Most High shall abide under the shadow of the Almighty."[21]

You and I are "in Him." There is a popular line from a hit movie that says, "You complete me." Our completeness is in Him.[22] Another verse says it this way: "We have known and believed the love that God has for us. God is love, and he who abides in love abides in God, and God in him."[23]

I can't think of a single born-again believer, who is in pursuit of

God relationally, who doesn't want to please Him. To not want to please God would be like a husband not wanting to please His wife, or a wife not wanting to please her husband. There's eventually going to be trouble in paradise in a relationship like that. It would be like an employee not wanting to please their boss. They might as well get their resume ready, and start looking for another job.

Whenever a person has a true relationship with God, there is a heart's desire to please Him. When you and I live in the expression of faith, we are releasing heaven on the earth, because faith is a heavenly substance—a substance whose origins are in an "unseen reality." Faith is a substance that is a part of the very DNA of God and heaven.

So when we live by faith—and the Bible says the just shall live by His faith[24]—then we are literally living the way God lives. This is why God is pleased. The truth is God has faith in us, so why wouldn't He expect faith from us?

"But without faith it is impossible to please Him, for he who comes to God must believe that He is, and that He is a rewarder of those who diligently seek Him."[25]

TAKE CONTROL

In our pursuits in life, we must learn to separate the important from the interesting. I'd much rather be on the offense instead of the defense. How about you? I'd rather have the ball, with a posture to advance, and the potential for scoring, instead of a posture to defend my goal line. Instead of having a wait and see approach to life...

"Life's been good so far..."

"We haven't dealt with very much adversity, but any minute now..."

I'd rather be living by faith, mixing it with proactive wisdoms from God, and getting ahead. I'd rather be in the driver's seat of my life, yielded to God and His plan for my life, than living aimlessly or in the wrong plan.

It's time to take control. Now is the time for the devil, our adversary, to be on the defense for a change. Intuitively, I've always known, this is the position and posture the believer is supposed to take. For maybe the first time ever, today's new believer has the opportunity to live aggressively, take territory from the enemy individually, and, as a corporate army, mobilize to bring destruction to darkness.

God's Word is very bold about this: "They will take up serpents; and if they drink anything deadly, it will by no means hurt them; they will lay hands on the sick, and they will recover."[26]

Satan and his allies throughout time have always been referred to in the Bible as snakes, serpents and scorpions. (You can read this in the account of the Garden of Eden in the book of Genesis.) So in

---

Embrace God's plan for your life. Say aloud, "Lord, I receive Your plan for my life. I receive the power of possibility to live it. Now, show it to me."

---

this verse I just mentioned, Jesus was telling us to handle our enemy instead of being handled by him—to control him, instead of being controlled by him. The purpose for sickness and the reason for lack and poverty is to control us. The singular assignment of brokenness is control. In other words, I can't give away something I don't possess myself, so if I'm broken, how can I heal and help the broken?

If someone sought to enter your house with the purpose of overtaking you, to control you and your family, would you allow it?

No, of course not. That's why we have locks on the door, alarm systems, and other means of protection. We've created a safety zone, where we personally control our environment and atmosphere!

Embrace God's plan for your life and take control. If you don't know what it is, declare it by faith. Say aloud, "Lord, I receive Your plan for my life. I receive the power of possibility to live it. Now, show it to me."

As He reveals Himself and His plan to you, mix faith and wisdom. Believe that there is a measure of faith for every step of your journey. Be today's believer and enjoy a better tomorrow.

CHAPTER 5

CONQUER YOUR AIRSPACE

THEN YOU'LL WIN THE WAR ON THE GROUND

With the understanding of mixing faith and wisdom, and how we need to take control from the devil for our lives, let's explore a mystery in scripture: "In which at one time you walked [habitually]. You were following the course and fashion of this world [were under the sway of the tendency of this present age], following the prince of the power of the air. [You were obedient to and under the control of] the [demon] spirit that still constantly works in the sons of disobedience [the careless, the rebellious, and the unbelieving, who go against the purposes of God]."[1]

What Paul is telling us is there is a battle for our own personal airspace, and the devil is the prince of the power of the air. He lives in the atmosphere. So if he can control your atmosphere—your airspace—then he can control the quality of your life, your family, your home, your office, and your church, if you allow him. What you allow in the atmosphere of your life is important.

Think of it this way: Strategically every military seeks to control the airspace of their enemy first, because if they have superior air

65

power, then they can control what happens on the ground. When we manifest peace, we control our atmosphere with this quality. We can literally influence our airspace with His rest. When we express peace, we create environment. That means we have to battle for supremacy of our atmosphere first—and win. Only then can we influence others to control their atmosphere purposefully to eventually create a new environment of their own.

What you allow in the atmosphere of your life is important.

Our warfare is not with people, even though that is the perception of many Christians. It is with "the power of the airspace"—and by controlling it we can create our own "compelling culture" rather than being led by the culture of the enemy.

BUILD YOUR OWN BUBBLE OF AIRSPACE

More than a decade ago, as I sat there glued to the television screen, along with millions of other people around the world, and watched the U.S. "shock and awe" air attacks on Baghdad, Iraq, I thought fervently about Ephesians 2:2—the verse I quoted at the beginning of this chapter. It's a well-known fact in "battle strategies" that the country that is the strongest militarily is the one who has a superior air force. This is why, when going to war, the first battle is to control the airspace of a country. Whoever controls the air has the upper hand—the ability to determine from the air the movement on the ground.

God said, "Our fight is not on the ground with flesh and blood. The real battle for the believer is in the air" (my paraphrase). Whoever controls the airspace—your airspace—ultimately determines the atmosphere and environment of your life. The choice is yours and mine!

So how do you do that?

One way is by what you say. Life and death are in the power of the tongue.[2] Your mouth releases power. This power creates your environment. It directly affects the atmosphere where you're living. You are literally building your own bubble of airspace by what's coming out of your mouth—and that airspace will determine not only the quantity of your days, but also the quality of your life.

You and I have our own personal battlefields, and we are warring over the control of our airspace. Since our adversary is "the prince of the power of the air," we must assault him by releasing a powerful

> *Whoever controls the airspace—your airspace —ultimately determines the atmosphere and environment of your life.*

force that will afflict him and push him back. This empowers us to gain control of the territory of our lives, so we can win back our environment. What unleashes this force is a relentless barrage of words that contain the power of possibility.

You can turn your circumstances around by taking back your atmosphere, by releasing the power of possibility out of your mouth. Start this today by:

- Stopping every negative word and speaking only positive words.
- Eliminating all complaining and griping, and turning your words into praise, thankfulness and gratitude to God.
- Consider the present—today—a gift. That's why it's called "present."

This will begin to change your surroundings slowly, not necessarily overnight. But in time, your airspace will be yours again.

CHANGE YOUR ENVIRONMENT

The Bible tells us that "a plan (environment) in the heart of a man is like deep water, but a man of understanding draws it out."[3] There's a "hidden environment" deep on the inside of you, and only understanding will draw it to the surface. As a man with a certain level of understanding, I'm speaking to what's already in you. The plans of God—His environment—have been deposited in the safe deposit box of God's people—their hearts or spirits—and it's time to withdraw those secret treasures, those hidden agendas and plans, that relate to your life in God. Then you can transcend your circumstances and experience greatness. This is what the "new believer today" does!

Since it takes understanding to draw out God's plans, how do you receive understanding? To help you, I've included a list of scriptures where God teaches us how (Appendix I). He gives us all the

The plans of God—His environment—have been deposited in the safe deposit box of God's people— their hearts or spirits—and it's time to withdraw those secret treasures, those hidden agendas and plans, that relate to your life in God.

details in His Word! I've also included a list of characteristics of a man or woman of understanding. I believe it will reveal even more of the power of understanding (Appendix II).

Whatever you're facing right now, no matter how numerous the challenges, how daunting the problems, how big the mountains, though it all seems impossible, God is giving you wisdoms—strategies—in this book to see your way out. Though your problems give you a sense of being held captive, Jesus came to set the captive free:

"The Spirit of the Lord is upon Me, Because He has anointed Me to preach the gospel to the poor; He has sent Me to heal the broken-hearted, to proclaim liberty to the captives."[4]

God and I want to bring deliverance to your captivity—to release you from your own personal emotional jail cell. We want you to begin to confront your issue. Go ahead, rattle the cage of your circumstances.

Why not now?

Why not today?

Why not here?

Why not you?

God hasn't given you worldly hope that's vain and powerless. He's given you heavenly hope and faith mixed with wisdoms—straight from His heavenly, eternal realm. They are for you to release

---

God hasn't given you worldly hope that's vain and powerless. He's given you heavenly hope and faith mixed with wisdoms—straight from His heavenly, eternal realm.

---

into and permeate the atmosphere of your life, therefore changing your environment.

This is one way you bring His heaven to your earth, His world to your experience, His existence to your reality. "Assuredly, I say to you, whatever you bind on earth will be bound in heaven, and whatever you loose on earth will be loosed in heaven."[5]

When you release your words of faith, then the God who is for you invades your emotional prison cell![6] He breaks in and breaks you out, but first, you must shake the bars with your faith!

Remember the story of Paul and Silas?

"The judges went along with the mob, had Paul and Silas's clothes ripped off and ordered a public beating. After beating them black-and-blue, they threw them into jail, telling the jail keeper to put them under heavy guard so there would be no chance of escape. He did just that—threw them into the maximum-security cell in the

---

When you release your words of faith, then the God who is for you invades your emotional prison cell!

---

jail and clamped leg irons on them. Along about midnight, Paul and Silas were at prayer and singing a robust hymn to God. The other prisoners couldn't believe their ears. Then, without warning, there was a huge earthquake! The jailhouse tottered, every door flew open, all the prisoners were loose."[7]

This isn't the first time God has created a prison break, and it's not the last...

In Jesus' Name, as today's believer and a voice of value in your life, I release the power of possibility into you and your captivity. I shake, rattle and shatter the bars that have held you as a prisoner. By faith, I break off the chains that have withheld you. I release you into your freedom now. The time has come. It's a prison-break. All four walls of limitation come down. The power of possibility has done it again. Welcome to a new level of freedom.

WISDOMS TO DEAL WITH ADVERSITY

As today's new believer, we must learn to respond positively to problems because our approach to resistance, trouble and difficulty determines whether we progressively move forward—or not.

As parents, we all want our children to win. I've never met a parent who wanted their child to lose. When my boys were younger, I had the joy of coaching with a friend of mine. Our sons played on the same baseball team together. Year after year, we made the playoffs, but when our sons lost, their "bad attitudes" quickly followed—and so did the attitudes of many of the parents. They would badmouth the umpire, "He robbed us of the game!" They'd poor-mouth the coaches. They'd speak badly about the playoff system.

When the kids bellyached, I knew they had learned this from their parents! This was the wrong approach to resistance, trouble and adversity. So we had to teach our team to lose gracefully. I had to stop practice on more than one occasion and tell my son when he struck-out, or got thrown out trying to take an extra base, "Huh uh,

---

Real peace is in walking with God, and working with Him.

---

no way you're going to pout. You're not going to talk back. You're not going to think you got cheated. No, you're not going to throw down your bat."

If we don't deal with even small disappointments the right way, then we teach our children the wrong response to trouble, resistance and problems. In essence, this is in epidemic proportions today, not only among our children, but also among many adults. They do not deal with adversity correctly. They don't know how to live by faith. Instead they reach for the escape button and eject into some sort of virtual comfort. Real peace is in walking with Him, and working with Him.[8] There's a reason why "He's the lily of the valley" and not the lily of the mountaintop.[9] It's because there is a rest available to every believer in the middle of turmoil and difficulty. There is a beauty you will discover in trouble that you will never experience on the mountaintop.

LEARN TO RESIST

Years ago, when our two eldest sons were 7 and 4, my mom came to Ft. Worth, Texas, where we were living, just to spend a week with us. She read devotions with the boys every day, played with them, cooked for us, and just hung out. It was heavenly for her to be in our home. She always carried a presence of God's greatness.

One day, as we were talking in the living room, the boys were in the playroom and started getting loud. We could tell there was a little scuffle going on. I jumped up to go referee the situation when

There is a rest available to every believer in the middle of turmoil and difficulty.

mom stopped me, "Scott, sit down, just let them work it out. It's good that they learn how to resolve conflict at this time in their lives, when the worst that could happen is a scratch or someone get knocked down."

I sat down, and, sure enough, a few minutes later, they had worked it out. How many times, do we send our kids to their own bedrooms, in the opposite ends of the house, when they get into conflict, instead of allowing them to grow through trouble? Why don't we allow them to resolve their own conflict?

If we did, maybe we wouldn't wonder why, when they're adults, they don't know how to deal with real resistance, problems and adversity.

God wants us to know how to deal with the challenges that come our way. He has given us a measure of faith and wisdoms to mix together to succeed. He has wisdom after wisdom in His word for us to apply to our lives.

He instructs us through the Apostle Peter: "Humble yourself under the mighty hand of God. Resist the devil and he will flee."[10] In this scripture, we are told to do two things. First, we are to position ourselves in humility by simply submitting to God's plan and ways. That's humbling ourselves under the mighty hand of God.

Second, we are to resist with the measure of faith we have for this specific problem. Then God's hand goes into action. He backhands the devil and "poof" he's gone. Now that's walking with Him and working with Him in the unforced rhythms of grace. That's teamwork.

But we must understand how to resist. As today's new believers, we are called to be a resistant force upon the earth. No, there's nothing new about that. This has always been a characteristic of a Christian that we must hold on to and take with us on our journey. This in many ways can be the difference between moving forward

> *God wants us to know how to deal with the challenges that come our way. He has given us a measure of faith and wisdoms to mix together to succeed.*

or sitting still. This is where people, including believers, get stuck in a cycle, living in a perpetual routine of sameness—one where they expect something for nothing—change—but without the proper actions to create a positive consequence.

Resistance simply starts with the perspective of "I may be right, I may be wrong, but God is always 100 percent right—all the time, always and forever." This mindset requires humility: "Humble yourself, under the mighty hand of God, resist the devil and he will flee."[11]

Resistance is automatic, when we choose humility, living with the viewpoint that God's Word is always 100 percent correct. This approach places us on God's path where the evil one has restricted access. He has no jurisdiction on God's highway. In fact, he is an outlaw.

When the devil was thrown out of heaven, it was the first time he'd ever felt the power of the mighty hand of God, and it left an indelible imprint on his mind. So when we demonstrate humility,

God didn't tell us to "say what we have," but that "we have what we say."

our enemy goes into "fleeing mode" knowing that the mighty hand of God cannot be too far behind.

The Bible says that Satan fell from heaven, like lightning from the sky. That must have hurt really badly! He has never forgotten. So when we submit to God's ways and thoughts, the devil starts looking over his shoulder. He knows God is near.

We resist in many ways, including with our words. Our sphere of resistance is expanded by what comes out our mouths. God didn't tell us to "say what we have," but that "we have what we say." Therefore, another form of humility is to say what God says we have, and who God says we are, even when our circumstances don't seem to line up with what He says.

He says, "Let the weak say I am strong."[12]

Why does God tell us to say something that seems like a lie? The same reason Jesus told Peter to get out of the boat. The implication was that he could walk on water, because Jesus was out walking on the water.

What is your situation? Does it seem impossible? God is into doing the impossible. Whatever your challenge is, it's no more impossible than walking on water. Every time we speak God's words, we manifest His force of life. We experience His life-giving power that automatically creates resistance to the force of death.

He tells us so in His Word: "For assuredly, I say to you, whoever says to this mountain, 'Be removed and be cast into the sea,' and does not doubt in his heart, but believes that those things he says will be done, he will have whatever he says."[13]

I understand your circumstantial mountain seems impossible and unmovable, but God says bring mountain-moving resistance to it, and it will fall into the sea. It will disappear. Your words have that kind of power if you believe. When you get one or two mountain victories under your belt, instead of being overshadowed by the next mountain, you'll overshadow that one through the bigness of God in you!

Another way you resist is by sowing seed. I'm a true believer in the principle of seed, then time, then harvest.[14] That the action of planting seeds will in time produce an event of increase—or harvest.

To get a desirable outcome in your life during troubled times, in the midst of adversity, you have to create a series of positive actions.

Sowing seed is sowing money or resources into what we often call "good ground." Good ground is soil—like a ministry or a person that bears fruit—into which you sow your resource—whether that resource is your time, talent, goods or money.

So to get a desirable outcome in your life during troubled times, in the midst of adversity, you have to create a series of positive actions, with one example being sowing seed. Actions like this produce a greater level of inner energy as well as build new strength.

If you don't take actions to build new strength, if you don't break out of the cycle of sameness, you will experience failure—like a meltdown. One translation says, "If you fall to pieces in a crisis, there wasn't much to you in the first place."[15]

Resistance through challenges can cause us to shut down. Sometimes the pressure of our circumstances is immense, but the enemy's very purpose for adversity is to produce a breakdown. The term "nervous breakdown" infers that a person had a flaw—an inner weakness—where they couldn't withstand the adversities of life. So that weakness caused them to buckle under the weight of it, produc-

As a believer, it's in your DNA to be a warrior.

ing failure. In reality, life is full of trouble, and we have to learn how to mix faith and wisdom to come out of it. Jesus said, "In the world, you'll have trouble, but be of good cheer, I've overcome the world."[16] Another translation says, "In this godless world you will continue to experience difficulties. But take heart! I've conquered the world."[17]

What good news! We could say: "He overcame a world full of trouble. So in overcoming the whole, the smaller part that was trouble was taken care of in the process." What I see in this statement is Jesus saying, "Trouble, problems, tribulations…they are really no big deal."

Of course when we're going through them, they feel big—huge like mountains. But later, in the rearview mirror, they are small.

Troubles come to break us down, but God's plan is to take the trouble that the devil purposed to bring us harm, and turn it for our good.

As a believer, it's in your DNA to be a warrior, to bring resistance, to lean against unrighteousness as light does to darkness that flees. However, that "warrior spirit," can also bring about great destruction to God's kingdom, the body of Christ and His house. I've recognized that many Christians don't know what to do with the "spirit of fight" that's in them. Oftentimes, they turn it on one another, doing the devil's work for him. But we are never to do that.

"For we do not wrestle against flesh and blood (people), but against principalities, against powers, against the rulers of the darkness of this age, against spiritual hosts of wickedness in the heavenly places."[18]

Fight for someone, never against anyone. It's easy to fight against things, but that's taking a defensive posture. To stay on the offensive, we have to always fight for something or someone. You are an overcomer and a winner![19]

ADVERSITY MAKES US BETTER

Missy is a gourmet cook. She comes by it honestly, as her mother, Mary Neece, affectionately called "Ma Dear," was a phenomenal cook. Missy is constantly gathering recipes, creating new sauces and combinations of spices and foods. We have a great time in the kitchen—her cooking and me eating. One evening she wanted to cook something with shrimp since she had read an enlightening article about them.

Not all things are good, but all things are working for our good.

The article read that shrimp raised in a pond with no predators and no currents require antibiotics mixed into the water to keep them healthy. The chef being quoted in the article went on to say that shrimp raised in a pond didn't satisfy his taste buds. They didn't have enough flavor. On the contrary, shrimp raised in the wild, those who face the challenges of currents and predators, need no antibiotics, no supplementation, and no artificial feeding. They are healthy in their natural habitat. They are not only better, but also much healthier for the consumer. He concluded by saying they have a much more flavorful taste.

How revealing. We are the same way. By persevering through adversity, we produce character, and through character, hope.[20]

The Bible encourages us: "And we know that all things work together for good to those who love God, to those who are the called according to His purpose."[21]

> *If we do what's appropriate in the middle of adversity, through a series of positive actions, we will break out and break into the new—whether that's a new level, a new place, a new experience or new success!*

The point is that not all things are good, but all things are working for our good. Your troubles are working for your good. They are producing new levels of strength in you, causing you to possess a greater level of power, so you can demonstrate His purpose on the earth.

We have to remember that we can't do the inappropriate thing in trouble or we will break down. But if we do what's appropriate in the middle of adversity, through a series of positive actions, we will break out and break into the new—whether that's a new level, a new place, a new experience or new success!

It was one thing for the children of Israel to break out of 430 years of captivity by the Egyptians. It was another thing for them to break into the Promised Land.

There are things that you may need to break out of today. Know this, you have a measure of faith for the break out. That crisis has been working for your good, creating new sources of power in you. Go ahead, rattle the cage and break out. The breakout was preparing you for the break-in. Now your newly discovered success has produced a new level of faith that will enable you to break into the promises of a new life!

Abraham broke out into the promise of God that had been postponed too long—a promise the Heavenly Father prophesied saying Abraham would become the father of many nations. For well over two decades, the Word of God was delayed, but Abraham staggered not in any unbelief at this promise from God.[22] When Isaac was born, the prophecy was fulfilled. God's promise came to pass. God not only had breakout in mind, but also He had the desire for Abraham to "break in" to a new life, a new level.

When you believe God and back it up with the appropriate actions, it becomes the supreme expression of your faith in God.

"Was not our forefather Abraham [shown to be] justified (made acceptable to God) by [his] works when he brought to the altar as an offering his [own] son Isaac? You see that [his] faith was cooperating with his works, and [his] faith was completed and reached its supreme expression [when he implemented it] by [good] works."[23]

Like Abraham, when you believe God and back it up with the appropriate actions, it becomes the supreme expression of your faith in God. You are not yesterday's believer.

So what will your new actions do for you?

What will the appropriate actions do for your marriage and family?

What will the correct actions do for your future?

What will the right actions, that validate your faith in God, do for His kingdom and your relationship with Him?

These correct actions of faith are simply the confirmation that you are today's believer—that you know how to mix faith and wisdom, the culmination of many moves of God, to produce a better tomorrow.

CHAPTER 6

GOD GETS YOU!

HE UNDERSTANDS YOU AND
HAS PERSONAL ANSWERS

Missy and I had been married just a few years when I was forced to deal with what was diagnosed as a life-threatening situation. We had just gotten back from Los Angeles when I became very ill. The symptoms were so gross, I will not elaborate on them in this book. As I pursued a cure of some sort, I began where I always had—with the Word, with my relationship with God.

After a few weeks, I realized my faith was weak. This sickness was taking a physical toll on my body, and I had lost 10 pounds in the process. I asked someone I trusted to lay hands on me and pray. I engaged my faith, but still there was no change.

I continued to lose weight. Four weeks into it, I had lost 20 pounds. As I sought answers, I went to the doctor. He diagnosed me with an intestinal parasite—something I had picked up traveling around the country. He prescribed a medicine designed to kill the parasite, but it didn't seem to make a difference. After taking the medicine for two days, I heard that inner voice say, "Don't take that medicine."

No, I wasn't delusional. It was the counsel of the Holy Spirit—that voice that rises up in our hearts and minds and guides us through life. I trust the Holy Spirit. I trust His counsel. Our bodies are the temples of the Holy Ghost, so surely He knows what's best for our bodies.[1] You listen to Him, too, and He will counsel you about your physical body. Our bodies are a shared responsibility with the Holy Spirit.

> *The counsel of the Holy Spirit is that voice that rises up in our hearts and minds and guides us through life.*

So even though my mind could not reason it out, I did what the voice told me to do. I had chosen to live this way many years before—to follow the counsel of the Holy Spirit in all situations. I flushed the meds down the toilet, knowing intuitively, it was right for me at that time in that situation.

Still continuing to pursue the natural—alongside the spiritual—I went to another doctor, an internal specialist. What followed was a series of humiliating tests. I went along with it even though in my heart I knew they were looking for a needle in a haystack. I knew that I was more in tune with my physical world than the experts. Their prognosis was concerning: "It had to be cancer."

From that day on, they aggressively continued sending me up the ladder to more specialists. By this time, I had lost over 35 pounds. My strength was gone and my faith was no longer focused on my healing. I focused what little faith I had left on hearing His voice.

Five months and more than 45 pounds lighter, as I walked into yet another doctor's office, I noticed the plaque beside the door.

It said his name, and underneath his name was the phrase, "Practicing Medicine." Instantly the Holy Spirit said inside me, "And they are practicing on you." As I slowly walked into the waiting room, "They are practicing on you," kept being replayed inside my head like an echo. I signed in, staying the course, not jumping ship midway through it, even though something was up. God was speaking to me and was about to give me new direction.

As I was seated, instantly, the Holy Spirit started speaking to me again: "Pick up that magazine."

OK, I thought as I picked up one in front of me and thumbed through it.

"Nope, next magazine."

Thumbed through it.

"Nope, three magazines beneath the top one."

I began thumbing through it, glancing at the headers in regard to the topics. As I did, He said, "You missed it. Go back five pages."

Sure enough. Down the side of a page was a short article that described about every symptom I had experienced. The topic was

---

Don't put your relationship with God in a box.
The power of possibility comes in many shapes
and sizes.

---

lactose intolerance—the inability to breakdown the sugar enzyme in milk. In the article, it even gave the remedy.

When this happened to me, it was the mid 80s, so lactose intolerance wasn't a household topic or nutritional sensation like today. No one talked about it, and there certainly weren't dairy-free drinks and foods readily available.

I knew I had found my answer. So I got up, walked out the door, went to the health food store, got my enzyme, thanked the Holy

Spirit, and started taking it. Three days later, I got my strength back. A week later, I was gaining weight. I never visited those doctors again. As they say, "The rest is history."

However, this physical challenge taught me something so significant about my relationship with God. His abilities, characteristics and solutions are infinite. His answers, cures and solutions come in many forms. So don't put your relationship with God in a box. The

> *The answers we want, the solutions we need, and the lifestyles of consistent success we desire are grounded in an intimate relationship with God.*

power of possibility comes in many shapes and sizes. And when we specify that something has to be a certain way, we may just miss the way in which He is resolving life's dramas.

The path in which He chose to take me during my crisis was to relationally engage with Him, to listen carefully to His voice. As you see by now, I'm no stranger to trouble, problems or tests. Each one of them has added wealth to my journey—and today I am rich beyond compare.

MEASURE YOUR FAITH

The answers we want, the solutions we need, and the lifestyles of consistent success we desire are grounded in an intimate relationship with God. I stated at the beginning of this book that my goal through these pages was to demonstrate for you the power of possibility way of living, the power of a mature relationship with God out of which you learn to use your faith to prevent future problems—as well as fix your existing ones.

I said that as you read many of my real-life encounters with God that have forever been imprinted in my mind and heart, you would see how God is not just a figure that I've read about in the Bible, but my relationship with Him has been made real through experiences with Him—and they produce what I need and want in my life and ministry.

That's what God desires for you. It's what Jesus yearns for you, and it's the Holy Spirit's purpose for your life as well. It's the power of possibility. It's how you can live so that what seems impossible in your life can suddenly become possible! This is God's quest for you. It's a journey of a lifetime full of adventure and joy.

The Bible tells us how God anointed Jesus of Nazareth with the Holy Spirit and with power, and how He went about doing good and healing all who were oppressed by the devil, because God was with Him.[2]

What does that mean?

Yes, Jesus' actions were good. His words produced results of healing, deliverance from captivity, and freedom for any individual who was bound. But what this really tells us is Jesus went from place to place with an offensive posture, an aggression to destroy anything that resembled the curse. He stalked negative forces that had plagued humanity for thousands of years. He became the predator instead of the prey, and regardless of what shape, type or form the curse took, it became His prey that He confronted with the unrelenting power of possibility.

The curse had no defense against His power, because good always overcomes bad.

In my parents' home, we were so busy fixing problems that it felt like we were consistently trying to simply keep our heads above water so we wouldn't drown.

As the new believers of today, our new reality shouldn't be just fixing problems. It should be preventing them! We shouldn't be the prey, but the predator who is going around overcoming evil with good.[3]

I have never quit living this way. It's the only way I know how to live—to purposefully pursue life. I've chosen to live more proactively by keeping the adversary retreating. That's what Jesus did. He said, "The wicked one is coming and he has nothing in me."[4] The devil couldn't place a demand on Jesus because he had nothing of himself in Jesus.

No fear...

No doubt...

No sin...

No unbelief...

> *Like Jesus, if we live life on purpose building a significant friendship with God, we will constantly be charging into the enemy's territory of darkness with the power of possibility.*

There was none of the devil's characteristics, thoughts or actions in Jesus that would allow the devil to affect Jesus' situations—until Jesus allowed the devil to at the end of His life. That was part of God's plan to defeat the devil. Jesus' crucifixion, death, burial and resurrection were God's plan to destroy Satan's power over mankind—and it worked.

Like Jesus, if we live life on purpose building a significant friendship with God, we will constantly be charging into the enemy's territory of darkness with the power of possibility. By being grounded deeply into our relationship with Him, when we enter hostile environments, we will carry such authority that our enemy will surrender to his defeat! With just you and God, you are an unstoppable majority!

We have to locate every disruption to our faith in God to determine where the possible disconnect might be. Our faith is measurable—able to grow from one level to the next. To know how we need to grow or increase our faith means we have to ask ourselves, "Where does my faith end?"

In the story of Shadrach, Meshach and Abednego, these Hebrew friends understood that the continual challenging of their faith showed them where their belief ended. If you'll read the story in the beginning chapters of Daniel, in the process of being punished for their faith, they encountered test after test that located where they were in their journey of faith:

- From the polite invitation to bow down before false gods…no, their faith was at least that big.
- To the threats they endured if they didn't bow down. Check—their faith stood that test.
- Then to the preparation of the punishment. I can see it now, their faith was being stretched.
- To being bound and all control taken from them, having no choice in the matter. Even then, their faith wasn't broken.
- When suddenly they were thrown into the fiery pit. The final faith response to their captors was, "Whatever, it doesn't matter. We believe God!"

This was an event that continued to escalate, that measured their faith. The three Hebrew men, as the scripture records, came back out of the fiery furnace without even the smell of smoke. They literally walked through fire and survived. What faith!

How far does your faith stretch? How much faith do you possess? What recent battle have you won by standing in faith and mixing it with wisdoms from God?

From having a faith that fixes problems to a faith that prevents them, this is our quest.

KNOW THE HIDDEN QUALITY

When Missy and I began BelieversWay Ministries and planted our first church, we built its foundation on Mark 9:23: "All things are possible to him who believes."

The Lord impressed upon me to raise up specialists—people with certain gifts and talents to create an environment of endless possibilities, an atmosphere of the supernatural!

> *We place a premium on understanding at BelieversWay because we realize it is in part what creates endless possibilities.*

The supernatural life is beyond the normal, beyond the routine, a departure from the forced grind of everyday life. It's a life of God putting His super—His anointing—on our natural ability and causing great things to happen in our lives. There are some people who are very uncomfortable with an environment like that, but they are the very people who have unanswered questions. They are the ones dealing with challenges, problems, dilemmas, and events beyond their control—and they need answers. They want to know why negative things are happening in their lives.

One of the greatest fears known to man is the fear of the unknown. Over the years, some of my greatest joys have come from the remarks people have made about Missy and me while helping them face the unknown. Stuck in a dilemma, unable to identify the source of their problems, which would give them some sort of comfort and solace, they have often said to us:

- "You explained my frustration and I'm over it now."
- "You demystified my problem, and the answer was right there all along. Thanks!"

• "I was confused about something, and you defined it in simple terms. I get it!"

When this happens, there is such a peace that washes over them. Confidence returns and courage fuels their ability to take on the next challenge of their personal journey.

So what was the hidden quality that was available—the one that worked to create a solution that resulted in wholeness? They gained understanding about their situation. When you understand, you move from being a passenger in life to sitting in the driver's seat with the steering wheel in your hand. Once again, you gain control.

Yes, God wants you to be in control. He's not the author of misunderstanding that produces confusion. This is why He said, "With all thy getting, get understanding."[5] So while you're out getting stuff, money, material things, and all the bling, don't forget the understanding. We place a premium on understanding at BelieversWay because we realize it is in part what creates endless possibilities.

God not only understands you, but also He speaks to you in a language you understand.

Your circumstance...your situation is speaking to you. Your problem is talking to you in a language you probably don't understand. And since it has its own unique tongue, many times you need someone to translate it for you. This is not uncommon, unusual or unique. It's as old as time.

WE ALL NEED TRANSLATORS

Even Pharaoh of Egypt discovered someone who could translate his misunderstood dreams—dreams that once interpreted defined the problem and were accompanied by a strategic wisdom that saved the known world.[6]

Pharaoh went in search of understanding and found the one translator in all of Egypt in a prison cell—Joseph.

Joseph had been a boy who had been betrayed by his family, sold into slavery, falsely accused of rape, and thrown into prison, but in every place he landed, he translated people's dreams, problems, circumstances and challenges accurately! I believe it was his ability to

---

God wants you to understand Him. That's why
He has invited you into a relationship with Him.

---

interpret his own realities that allowed him to stay the course to his purposed destiny. Everywhere he went he eliminated confusion and chaotic turmoil through understanding! He was a specialist!

God not only understands you, but also He speaks to you in a language you understand. Yes, God has someone who speaks your language—someone who can transport you from the unknown to the known.

If you've ever been misunderstood, you know the feelings of frustration that accompany it. Take heart, God has been misunderstood many times because He's been misrepresented. God wants you to understand Him. That's why He has invited you into a relationship with Him.

In fact, the creation of the world and mankind were for the purpose of man understanding God: "For since the creation of the world God's invisible qualities—His eternal power and divine nature—have been clearly seen, being understood from what has been made, so that people are without excuse."[7]

So the unseen reality has been made visible in creation through you and me collectively so the unsaved can understand the characteristics, qualities and nature of God.

The very earth and universe is one of God's interpreters. God doesn't want to be misunderstood.

The Bible is another tool God gave us to understand Him as well: "In the beginning was the Word, and the Word was with God, and the Word was God. He was in the beginning with God. All things were made through Him, and without Him nothing was made that was made."[8]

God made the Word available at a great cost, a very high price, for our understanding of Him. He gave us the life of Jesus to give us

---

God gets you! And He likes you!

---

even more understanding: "And the Word became flesh and dwelt among us, and we beheld His glory, the glory as of the only begotten of the Father, full of grace and truth."[9]

Jesus went about as a translator, an interpreter of lives, to explain people to themselves and in turn tell them, "God gets you. He's located you. He has targeted you because He knows you and wants to be known by you."

How does that make you feel? What a loving God! He gets you! And He likes you! He wants to know you—and be known by you. He wants relationship, and through that relationship He can help you develop the measure of faith He's deposited in you. Through relationship, He can grow you, make you whole, and lead you to living on the offense instead of the defense.

HE WANTS YOU TO KNOW HIM

One day, as recorded in The New Testament, Jesus had a dialogue with a woman at a well as a translator.[10] He told her all there was to know about her life. He recounted all the men she'd had intimate relationships with, and included her current companion was not her husband. As He read her mail, He interpreted her life. He helped her and imparted to her. "Then, leaving her water jar, the woman went back to the town and said to the people, 'Come, see a man who told me everything I ever did. Could this be the Messiah?'"[11]

Yes, sir! That's Him, the translator. "Come and meet a man who told me everything I ever did." Jesus was into interpreting people's problems, troubles and lives. His purpose was to eliminate the internal chaos that was resident in confusion, and present in a lack of understanding.

> *The emotions of being understood are priceless.*
> *Being understood is a value that every person*
> *in the world, whether consciously or not, needs*
> *above everything else.*

BelieversWay is one more tool God uses to bring understanding to His people. "God is not the author of confusion."[12] He wants the misunderstandings in people's lives to cease.

Years ago, there was a woman attending one of our campuses. Every time I saw her, she had a frown on her face. If I engaged in conversation with her, she would always talk about her past and what wasn't working in her life. She had a deep-seeded level of confusion.

During a special meeting we were hosting, she was present with the same sad countenance and low self-esteem as always. After the service, I went to her and interpreted her life, and to my amazement, the Holy Spirit told me to pray for her to have seven days of unbridled joy. He was talking about His joy—joy unspeakable and full of glory.[13]

Now, I always just do what the Holy Spirit says, so I told her, "Now I'm going to pray for you to have seven days of joy. You don't have to earn it or work for it. God gets you—He's searched you out.

He's targeted you and locked on to you. He wants you to know He knows you. Now it's time for you to experience Him. Just receive."

I laid hands on her and released the power of possibility.

Well, she received it. For the next seven days, she was giddy, bouncing off the walls. She was funny and full of laughter. Her countenance completely changed. The rain cloud above her head disappeared. This woman had experienced the power of possibility and joy was the result. God interpreted her life to her and removed the confusion. It was her new beginning of endless possibilities.

When the woman at the well experienced Jesus, she enthusiastically told her whole community about Him. For the next few days, Jesus interpreted everyone's lives—their past, present and future, showing them their potential and purpose.

> *God gave us the language of faith, because He wants you and I to know His culture and His dialect.*

"And because of His words many more became believers. They said to the woman, 'We no longer believe just because of what you said; now we have heard for ourselves, and we know that this man really is the Savior of the world.'"[14]

They said we believe, because He has eliminated our misunderstanding, removed our confusion, our randomness and all chaos from our lives.

This one woman, who experienced the power of possibility through a relational exchange with Jesus, created a series of events that produced endless possibilities to a city of people who encountered an interpreter.

The emotions of being understood are priceless. Being understood is a value that every person in the world, whether consciously or not, needs above everything else. Jesus came to the Earth to understand us, and, through the transaction of relationship, helps us to understand God.

God didn't give us the language of faith to complicate our lives as believers, to rob us of understanding, to create confusion, or to become a divisional element between His people. If that were so,

> *God's invitation to you is to enter a culture of understanding, where an environment exists of endless possibilities.*

He would be the author of confusion and division, and that would be a contradiction of who He is. No, God gave us the language of faith, because just like He who knows our language, He wants you and I to know His culture and His dialect. Authentic relationship is a two-way street. God deserves our pursuit of understanding Him. He deserves our understanding of His language—and He speaks the language of faith.

God so gets you today. He sees right through you, and what He sees doesn't surprise Him at all. He's targeted you for the purpose of getting to know you better, to explain you to you, to interpret your circumstances, to define your current problems—so that His understanding of you can wash over your emotions and bring wholeness to your inner-self.

Some of you are experiencing God as you read this. You feel like there are butterflies in your stomach. Your heart's speeding up. Your stomach is in your throat. That's the tangible touch of an interpreter. It's God touching you saying, "Tag, you're it! No, you don't get it. You're it. You're special. You're valuable. You're My prized possession. I understand you. That's why I love you. Now, come to Me. Get away with Me and you'll recover your life. Walk with Me. Work with Me in the unforced rhythms of grace. Watch how I do it."[15]

God is beyond bilingual. He's multilingual. He knows every tribe, culture and tongue. He speaks to every person in his or her own individual language as an interpreter of understanding. He talks the language that is our hearts' desires because we all want to understand. He gets you! And He has personal answers for your life.

In exchange, He asks only one thing—to understand Him! This is His invitation to you to enter a culture of understanding, where an environment exists of endless possibilities.

CHAPTER 7

Transition—No Man's Land

God's Ways to Get You Through Change

Transition is an interesting time in the life of a person's family or organization that can create extreme difficulty. It's when we find ourselves in between two points. Those obvious times in life are...

- From boy to man
- From girl to woman
- From unmarried to married
- From married to divorced
- Moving from one city to another
- Changing from one job to another

It's a moment that is indistinguishable. There was a point in The New Testament when Paul was neither Saul of Tarsus—who he was before becoming a Christian—nor was he Paul the Apostle—who he later became. There was a time in The Old Testament when Moses wasn't the son of Pharaoh, and neither was he the deliverer of God's people. When Jesus spent 40 days in the wilderness, He was in transition. After John the Baptist baptized Him, He left transition behind.

One of life's greatest challenges is that period of transition, that in-between time, that place of "no man's land." The problem is that during this kind of season, we are often unable to find clear precise direction. The result is we experience the missing link of understanding.

The drama and downfall of transition, when people are directionless, is that they will follow anyone. Too often, the loudest and

In the season of transition, be careful whom you follow, whose voice in which you place value.

most vocal person, by their sheer ability of being a know-it-all, takes the lead as the loudest voice in your life during transition. That is not good!

If you've ever been to a ballgame, and sat next to the guy who appointed himself as the play-by-play announcer, who questioned the umpire's every call, who had something to say about everything— yes, the obnoxious one—that's the person people typically follow when they are in transition. Now this individual is not necessarily the smartest or the wisest, but they are the loudest. For many, no man's land is a defining moment where decisions are made that have life-everlasting consequences.

In the season of transition, be careful whom you follow, whose voice in which you place value. If they are not living by faith, with a certain degree of understanding, respect them, but don't necessarily follow their advice. Everyone has an opinion, but much of it is based on things they haven't figured out yet. Jesus called this "the blind leading the blind."[1]

When you're in no man's land, follow God. Again, if we can prevent the problem, we won't have to go back and fix the consequences of wrong decisions.

STRATEGIES FOR MOVING OUT OF TRANSITION

When I am in transition, I have learned strategies to keep me moving forward and eventually out of that season. These have helped me stay the course and not be pulled in a wrong direction.

First, I praise Him. I bless the Lord at all times. His praise is continually upon my lips.[2] My praise silences all the other voices and maximizes His voice. Praise is a weapon that quiets our enemy, immobilizes him, keeps him at a distance, and turns his volume down. Praise assaults any enemy in our airspace, and like I've taught you, by winning our atmosphere we begin to influence our environment.

Second, I read and speak the Word aloud. This is God's strategy to build our faith. The Word instructs us that "faith *comes* by hearing, and hearing by the word of God."[3]

Praise is a weapon that quiets our enemy, immobilizes him, keeps him at a distance, and turns his volume down.

You'll need faith in God to believe what you're hearing. As His direction and guidance comes, a newly discovered energy will accompany it. That energy is encapsulated in the revelation of what He's showing you. It will illuminate you and shine on your path. Listen as God speaks through others who are loyal to Him, who are full of faith with Christ's characteristics. Ignore those who are simply personalities—empty and faithless.

As you engage in these daily activities, your life will be redefined. You'll be living as a today's believer. You'll walk as a new species of being. When we're born again, the old is gone, the new has come.[4] Allow transformation to take place in you, on you, through you and for you. Allow your mindsets to change. Let your thought processes change by being open to think things you've never thought before. Be more optimistic and let pessimism and negativity be things of the past. Endeavor to focus on what you have in your life—not on what you don't have. Recognize Whom

---

Giving unlocks your future and always opens your heart to hear.

---

you're praising, what you're reading, and what you're speaking are creating a new atmosphere in your life. The new things that you are doing are attracting new results in your world. Stay on that path.

YOUR NEXT MOVE

In no man's land, it's normal to be in a fog and be confused. There is a battle for supremacy. It's a war between the way things have been and the way they will be. But as your environment gradually changes—from executing the strategies I've explained—others will recognize the change in you probably even before you do. It's confirmation that the process is working.

Now, your next move in breaking through transition to the other side will be your giving. Your gifts—seed you sow—will assist in pulling you through into the new as well as pulling you out of the old. I explained this to some extent in Chapter 2 when I shared about one of our sons being healed from TB, and when I explained seedtime and harvest.

Giving unlocks your future and always opens your heart to hear. So ask the Lord, "What do you want me to give? Where do you want me to give?" He does want you to sow seed, so ask Him where to sow it. You want it in good ground that bears fruit.

Over the years, as countless numbers of people have asked me for prayer regarding their finances, the first question I always ask is, "Do you give systematically? Do you tithe systematically, or just when you have a little extra, or when a need moves you emotionally?"

I have found that more than 95 percent of the people who are in financial lack only give occasionally. Those types of Christians will continue to face financial challenges. As long as they don't tithe and sow consistently, they will be stuck in financial no man's land. They will be paralyzed—immobilized—with never enough.

Believers, we need to keep our money in motion, give habitually, and make it a routine. Your consistent giving will expedite your process through no man's land.

God's Word says, "There is that scattereth, and yet increaseth; and there is that withholdeth more than is meet, but it tendeth to poverty."[5]

Keep your money in motion, give habitually, and make it a routine. Your consistent giving will expedite your process through no man's land.

Another translation of this same verse reads, "The world of the generous gets larger and larger; the world of the stingy gets smaller and smaller."[6]

Giving is a very significant step in the process of moving through transition to the other side. Throughout the years, I've had people who wanted me to be responsible for their healing, prosperity, financial increase, and even their very lives—but without giving me the power to change their thinking, behavior, attitudes and choices. I absolutely refuse that responsibility. But give me the power to change these areas of your life and I guarantee your success.

God always confirms His Word[7] and He watches over it to perform it.[8] His words in our mouth will go forth and accomplish what we send them to do.[9]

In no man's land, whatever you do, don't withhold or it will close your heart. Live with open hands and you'll live with an open heart and soul. The seed in your life that you give today will affect progress, and determine your future. Great things happen here!

CHAPTER 8

SIMPLIFY YOUR LIFE—BUT STAY IN MOTION

NAVIGATING BETWEEN "GO" AND "YOU'VE ARRIVED"

Another strategy God has for you is to simplify your life. Think about it. Where is your life complicated? When life becomes a blur, and everything is going 100 miles a second, it's time to take matters into your own hands. The world is a forced rhythm. It's structured to run us to death. So we have to take control and slow things down.

I know when our boys were younger, because they were different ages, we would always check the schedule of the sports they desired to play because we couldn't be in three places at once. Our family rule of thumb was that one would have to play another sport that started at a different time of the year. We had to alternate schedules, and if any schedule ever conflicted with church, we didn't participate. God's house was always our number one priority. We couldn't let the world's forced rhythm wear us down.

God's grace has an unforced rhythm. It gives us choices, but doesn't put its thumb on us. That's not God's nature. There's simplicity in Christ, and we're to model our lives after that flow.[1] So, simplify your schedule and build pauses into it—moments where you can slow down and live. Get rid of the heavy and burdensome things that weigh your life down. "Throw off every weight, sin that so easily besets you so you can run the race that is set before you."[2]

You may be in transition today, but you don't have to stay there.

Throw off unnecessary things. If you allow others to dictate your every move, then you'll wind up living a life of their making with no one to blame but yourself. Take the time to build moments of excitement, adventure, spontaneity and fun.

You may be in transition today, but you don't have to stay there. You know change is necessary, so make it happen. Begin a lifestyle of consistency—consistently praising, reading and speaking His Word, giving, and simplifying your life. God gets you! And He is getting His answers to you!

ANSWERS COME WHEN WE LIVE IN FORWARD MOTION

Missy and I have never had a "wait and see" approach to life or to what God has called us to do. We've taken what God has spoken and purposefully brought it out of the world of words and thoughts and into this seen reality. When God gave us a specific plan for our ministry we followed it:

I've called you...to the great plains of Texas

...to the mountains of Colorado

...northward to the Canadian Border

...then to the world, you've been sent to the world.

That was our directive from God that He gave us in 1998. So we planted our first church in Amarillo, Texas, our second in Vail, Colorado, and our third in Midland, Texas. Because the apostolic anointing loves to start new things and plant, the power of possibility shows up, and every service produces endless possibilities.

A couple of years ago, because things were going so well in our campuses, we set out to begin a fourth campus and possibly move the headquarters of our ministry to Denver, Colorado. We gathered our staff and went to Denver for a time of vision casting, inspiration and planning. A few days into it, it seemed everyone was on board, but things weren't exactly right.

When we got back home, over the next few weeks, as we continued forward and made several trips back to Denver checking into facilities, looking for confirmation of our movement and direction, nothing happened. I mean nothing. The doors just didn't open! Months later, after not opening a campus in Denver and resolving that we weren't supposed to, the Lord said, "You've planted three churches, but planting and building are two different things. Build the churches you already have."

Whether you know it or not, you're where you are today because God opened a door for your life.

At first, when the door in the Denver community didn't open, I was perplexed. Why is this happening to me? Then I began to study Paul's journey in The New Testament and realized he had figured some things out that I was just beginning to experience about doors of opportunity.

Whether you know it or not, you're where you are today because God opened a door for your life. Jesus is the doorkeeper.[3] He opens and shuts doors. My personal journey has produced an understanding of how this works.

How can I know the will of God? How does God lead me? In part because of the doors He opens in our lives.

God's Word tells us: "Don't copy the behavior and customs of this world, but let God transform you into a new person by changing the way you think. Then you will learn to know God's will for you, which is good and pleasing and perfect."[4] Transformation begins by changing the way we think. That's how we learn God's will, so let the transformation begin.

God is drawn to motion. He is attracted into anyone's life who is in progressive motion.

Jesus told a story about people in forward motion—but it wasn't the right kind of motion. It reveals much to us:

"Yes. For there was once a man who threw a great dinner party and invited many. When it was time for dinner, he sent out his servant to the invited guests, saying, 'Come on in; the food's on the table.' Then they all began to beg off, one after another making excuses. The first said, 'I bought a piece of property and need to look it over. Send my regrets.' Another said, 'I just bought five teams of oxen, and I really need to check them out. Send my regrets.' And yet another said, 'I just got married and need to get home to my wife.'"[5]

God is drawn to motion. He is attracted into anyone's life who is in progressive motion.

In this story, Jesus gives us a snapshot of how God approaches people. He moves toward those in motion first. He first invited to His banquet a person who bought a piece of property, then another who bought a team of work animals, then another who just married.

God is attracted to people's movement, not those who intend to get in motion, but those who are movers and shakers, leaders, business people. When people already have the disciplines of moving life forward, that's one less thing God has to talk to them about.

Be one of those people for God! Get off the sidelines, out of the bleachers, and get in the game! That's where God's heart is, where people are.

In fact, God doesn't really get involved in our lives until we are in fluid motion. How can He work with someone who won't even get up and move?

> *God is attracted to people's movement, not those*
> *who intend to get in motion.*

His word reveals this: "Many are the plans of a man, but God directs his steps."[6] God directs progressive movement. So one form of God's direction is guiding our steps. You can't have steps if you aren't in motion. Now, if our relationship with God is isolated, meaning we don't move without a sign, a word, a prophecy, a dream, or a vision, and only then will we step out, do something, help, serve, or support, then we aren't people in motion to whom He's attracted.

I do my very best to stay in motion. I do not live with a mindset of where I'm waiting on God to move before I do. That's not God's thinking. He always wants us to move first. He says:

"Draw nigh to God, He will draw nigh to you."[7]

Who went first?

"Give then it will be given to you."[8]

Again, who goes first?

The new normal for today's believer is to stay in constant motion. At BelieversWay we say it like this, "I move, God moves, I move, God moves, I move, God moves."

God confirms this over and over in His word: "The footsteps of a righteous man are ordered of the Lord."[9] Footsteps are in motion. You can't stand still and have footsteps.

Yes, I believe God can guide by dreams, visions, supernatural encounters and events, but I believe that's not the norm. That's why it says, "These signs shall follow them that believe."[10] Signs aren't

---

"The footsteps of a righteous man are ordered of the Lord."[9] Footsteps are in motion. You can't stand still and have footsteps.

---

supposed to lead us, but be like a wake behind a boat. They follow as confirmation of our conversational relationship with God. Therefore, we must determine not to seek a sign for guidance.

Jesus said, "A wicked and perverse generation seeks a sign."[11] I don't want to over-spiritualize this, but as believers, it's something we should understand. Many Christians live their lives waiting to be led by a sign, a prophecy, a directive, a dream, or a word. Their thinking is, *When the Lord tells me to, then I'll do it!*

HE GUIDES US WITH PREVENTION

Another more simple form of God's direction is by prevention—when He prevents us from doing certain things. That's how our Denver church plant evolved, because as we pursued that direction, doors never opened. When God commissioned Paul to go out and preach, it probably felt a little like hit and miss to Paul. Here's a portion of his travels:

"Next Paul and Silas traveled through the area of Phrygia [Phrygia] and Galatia, because the Holy Spirit had prevented them from preaching the word in the province of Asia at that time. Then coming to the borders of Mysia [My-sia], they headed north for the province of Bithynia [Bi-thy-nia], but again the Spirit of Jesus did not allow them to go there. So instead, they went on through Mysia to the seaport of Troas [Tro-as]. That night Paul had a vision: A man from Macedonia in northern Greece was standing there, pleading with him, 'Come over to Macedonia and help us! So we decided to leave for Macedonia at once, having concluded that God was calling us to preach the Good News there.'"[12]

Like the disciples, Jesus had commissioned Paul to take the gospel to every nation. Paul is a church planter—a church builder. He is constantly in motion, getting on with his life. Paul is planting churches and building churches. He is constantly trying to enter countries. And what he's finding is that God is preventing him from going certain places. It doesn't say how. It just says he's forbidden to go there. The only time scripture gives us a clue about this is: The Spirit of Jesus kept him out of Asia.[13]

Prevention is one of God's tools for guiding us.

Unlike some Christians, Paul did not make this prevention an issue with God:

- "Lord, why are you telling me, 'No?'"
- "Why can't I go there?"

Paul's response was mature and confident in God. His attitude was: "Cool, I'll move on!"

Paul's thinking interpreted that "no" must be for my own good. We must let God's "no" be our guidance. Prevention is one of God's tools for guiding us.

When Jesus sent the disciples out by two's, He said: "Whatever towns or villages you go to, if they receive you, then good. But if they don't receive you 'shake the dust from off of your feet and move on.'"[14]

In other words, every "no" is telling you not to stay there, so keep moving! The "no" isn't to get us asking God "Why?" The "no" is to keep us in motion. If every time we experience resistance about what we want to do, we seek a dream, a prophecy, or some counsel, it's because we don't understand God will bring "no's" into our lives as well as "yes's." The "no" God gave us about planting a fourth campus was also a "yes" to focus on building the ones we had.

If we camp out at the "no," then we'll get an attitude about "no." And we'll start trying to force God to change His mind. When God closed that door, He was simply saying, "I have an open door of opportunity down the path. Just keep going."

BABY GATES AND BLOCKERS

When our boys were toddlers, we bought "baby gates" that we wedged in doorways to prevent them from going into certain rooms in the house. We wanted to protect them from objects that could hurt them, and from objects they could break.

They didn't stand at the gate crying saying, "Daddy, why, why, why?"

> *God's prevention is moving me toward His permission. My constant motion is moving me toward open doors of endless possibilities.*

No, they got it pretty quickly that access was denied. So their attention became preoccupied with the rooms in the house where they could freely roam and play.

Paul was OK with the baby gate, too. When God blocked him from entering certain places, he said, "Ok, it's not there. It's not there. It's not there. It's not there. Good. We must be getting closer to a "green light," closer to a "yes."

Why didn't the Holy Spirit tell Paul about Greece before he tried to enter three other countries? God wasn't guiding him by permission, He was guiding Paul by prevention. Paul believed if

110

the door was shut—that was "no." His viewpoint was "I'll just keep moving on instead of sitting here, beating my brains out trying to open it or trying to figure out why it's a 'no.' 'No' is a 'no!' Just keep moving."

I like Paul's perspective. It's healthy. It's confident. It trusts God implicitly and it keeps us in motion. It's become a very simple answer in my life that's helped me understand my relationship with God.

God guides by what He prevents. Yes, God can guide by other means like a prophecy, vision, dream, or a word. But it doesn't have to be that way every time, and we shouldn't require that of God. We shouldn't put Him in a box through false expectations.

I'm in cooperation with God. We collaborate on many details of life. I've learned that if He sends me a word, it's not the cake, it's the icing on the cake. Over the years, I've learned that God's prevention is moving me toward His permission. My constant motion is moving me toward open doors of endless possibilities.

THE DISTANCE BETWEEN "GO" AND "YOU'VE ARRIVED"

Certainly, Paul was guided by dreams and visions, but these weren't normal occurrences. We mean well when we look to Paul as an example of what we are to do in every situation, but many years lapsed between when God told Paul to do something and the next time God spoke to him. There was a distance—a span of time—between when God told Paul to do something, and when he arrived at the destination.

How many times have you heard from God, and then didn't again for a long time? It makes you question if you know how to hear from God at all. Imagine how Paul felt!

When God told him to go to Rome and stand before Caesar, it was several years later before he finally got there—and during that time he experienced shipwrecks, two assassination attempts, several trials, and a deadly snakebite.

It was a tough few years—with no communication during all those events. If Paul had been following signs, he could have easily turned way off course! I know most people would have.

While Paul made his way to Rome—for those few years—every time one of those obstacles arose, he didn't stop and say, "Lord, you told me to go to Rome. I've had problems ever since I've started this trip. I'm not sure, Lord. Maybe I'm not supposed to. Maybe I heard you wrong. Give me a sign, Lord!"

No, Paul didn't live that way. He didn't act that way. But some Christians do. They think, *I can't move until God points and launches me towards a particular goal. I'll join the prayer team, if you tell me to. I'll tithe, if you tell me to Lord. I'll serve, if you give me a sign.*

> *If you fall, get up and brush yourself off. If you fall again, get up again. If you fall again, get up again.*

We are in a relationship with the one and only true God. He is our Father. So we must start living by moving and getting involved. Yes, we will experience ups and downs. The tests, trials, peaks and valleys all come with living everyday life. But the Word encourages us that "The steps of a good man are ordered of the Lord, tho' he falls, he will not stay down."[15]

If you fall, get up and brush yourself off. If you fall again, get up again. If you fall again, get up again. This is how life is and it's OK!

You mean, even if God directs my steps, I might fall?

Yes.

That should be a relief to some of you who are like me—I have fallen in pursuit of a goal more than once or twice. But I got back up and went at it again.

If you fall, nothing's wrong! Get up! It's OK. Just get up and go at it again. Paul said, "You're falling, stumbling as you're apprehending the thing that you've been apprehended for."[16]

Sometimes in the midst of reaching for something, we don't quite make it, and we fall. Rather than fall apart, we're simply supposed to get back up and continue reaching for it.

Be Faithful—No Matter What The Journey Is Like

God wants us to be faithful—through all the directives, failures, highs and lows. He wants us to be faithful when we're hearing amazing things from Him, and when it seems someone has cut the line of communication. It takes a mature relationship with God to keep going—and in the right direction—but that is our heart's desire, isn't it? I know it's mine. I love God with all my heart and soul, and no matter what, I will keep moving forward with all He's told me to do, with all that I know to do. I trust Him to close doors and stop me if I'm reaching in the wrong direction. He loves me—and you! He's watching over us and our paths.

I remember after I graduated from high school, I took a road trip with a group of friends. For a few weeks we drove through the Rocky Mountains of Colorado, Utah and Idaho. Our last stop was Wyoming, home of Yellowstone National Park. As we drove up to the lodge and took it all in, about 200 yards away was the famous geyser Old Faithful. Hundreds of people were staring at this hole in the ground. We walked over to the viewing area and waited about 15 minutes.

Right on cue, Old Faithful blew. I heard a gentleman say: "You could set your watch by it."

Millions of people visit there each year to view Old Faithful. Why?

Because people are hungry for faithfulness. Like God, people admire faithfulness, and it's faithfulness that creates a perpetual cycle of endless possibilities. Husbands want faithful wives. Wives want faithful husbands. Children want parents who are faithful to each other. Employees desire faithful bosses. Owners of businesses look for faithful employees. We all want faithful family members. We all want faithful friends—people we can genuinely trust. We want to know our reputation is safe in their hands. We want to know

> *Like God, people admire faithfulness, and it's faithfulness that creates a perpetual cycle of endless possibilities.*

they are an ally instead of an enemy—and that they'll stand up and defend our honor! We all desire faithful leaders, presidents, teachers and pastors—even a faithful God. As a pastor, it's a dream-come-true to have a church full of faithful people. Without faithfulness, we can't trust.

Don't disqualify yourself from the conversation because faithfulness sounds like an old school word, or because you think you are faithful, or even if you have been unfaithful, and you're living with the memory of that event and dealing with the consequences of your choices.

Faithfulness is a character quality that is timeless: "Moreover, it is [essentially] required of stewards that a man should be found faithful [proving himself worthy of trust]."[17]

Why does God require faithfulness? Because when someone is unfaithful, they break the bond of trust—and trust is the mortar that keeps relationships together.

As we're faithful to God, we are faithful to His processes when we use His ways and means, and it is evident in our lives. The circumstantial evidence backs up what we say.

Faithfulness is a heavenly expression that triggers endless possibilities in our lives.

For example, someone you know may have told you that they trust God. Well, OK, "God is faithful and trustworthy," but the issue really is: "Can God trust them?" If failure is not an option when it comes to our relationship with God, then we must be faithful to Him as well.

Faithfulness is a heavenly expression that triggers endless possibilities in our lives. If we don't want to drift, and we want to keep a current, up-close-and-personal relationship with God...with His Word...with His Spirit...then we have to be faithful.

God wants us to know exactly where we are in our relationship with Him—and that can be proven by our faithfulness. Our faithfulness can be measured by our pursuit of His ways, how our character remains steady, and if our affection stays turned toward Him and His causes. God takes all the guesswork out of what faithfulness means.

So how faithful are you? Look around. God uses the evidential confirmation experienced in our circumstances to affirm us and encourage us. Can you tell on what level God trusts you? Has He trusted you with much or little?

Faithfulness Yields Blessing

I liken it to when our boys were younger, and many times we would be in deep conversations with guests who were at our house. As they would walk by the room where we were talking, I'd stop the conversation until the boys passed. The truth is I didn't trust my children with adult levels of information. I was actually protecting them from knowledge for which they didn't and couldn't be responsible. Knowledge is power, and I knew as a parent that they couldn't handle much. So I protected the trust, knowing they had limits.

God is the same way. He is a great parent who will guard your ability to be faithful. And as we ascend from one level of faithfulness to the next, we break out into new levels of blessing. He tells us: "A faithful man will abound with blessings, But he who makes haste to be rich will not go unpunished."[18]

If you are faithful, you will abound with blessing.

If you are faithful, you will abound with blessing. Abound means "fully supplied, plenty, great quantity and flow." As we cultivate a faithful relationship with God and people, we will have great quantities of the blessing.

Now "God's blessing" is not the actual stuff, material wealth or extravagant possessions, but His blessing does create those things. The blessing of God in our lives releases the creative forces of the power of possibility (faith) to bring riches into our world, and "the blessing of the Lord brings wealth, without painful toil for it."[19]

Sound, steady faithfulness creates greater degrees of the blessing which brings wealth. Through our transactions of faithfulness—like a momentum that builds with each action—a tipping point is reached that trips the circuit, and then heavenly blessings are released creating riches. In other words, as we grow, the blessings grow. As we continue to be faithful, the blessings continue to come—and eventually we are abounding with blessings.

God's ways are processes that produce encounters and events that are on the side of the spectacular. They create endless possibilities where the sky is the limit.

Our vision at BelieversWay Ministries is to build each generation to reach the next through the power of relationship. That's our mission statement and our passion. The New Testament speaks of

---

Trust God and the last directive He gave you.
Keep moving forward.

---

relationship more than any other topic. It's a relational letter from God to all believers—not a book of laws, or do's and don'ts. So what God does in our generation—what God does in your life—the doors of endless possibilities He opens—will be directly related to our cooperation and participation. It will be directly related to your faithfulness to Him—and others.

God is faithful to you. He wants to get answers to you. He wants to help you navigate those emotions, events and challenges between "Go" and "You've arrived." Use the strategies explained in this chapter. Simplify your life. Build pauses into your race. Trust God and the last directive He gave you. Keep moving forward. God can work with you and for you when you're in motion.

CHAPTER 9

LISTEN TO THE MESSENGER

GOD HAS ONE FOR YOU

God has strategies to get you from where you are to where you want to be. He has strategies for you to experience the power of possibility and see the manifestation of your faith. Another one of those strategies is to connect you to a messenger—a preacher—who can speak into your life what God wants you to get and understand. A preacher is anointed to help develop your faith so you can access the power of possibility to overcome what seems impossible.

How many times have the words a pastor spoke inspired you to be courageous, have hope or know what decision you were to make? The purpose of the pastor—or preacher, teacher, messenger, or whatever your denomination calls him or her—is to give you something to hear, because faith comes by hearing, so that the power of possibility can be released into your life.

As a pastor, I know what the fruit of this is like. I've seen people act in response to what I said, and their actions forever changed their lives. Being a pastor, speaking the words God gives me in my study time, prayer time and as I go along in life is what I've always known I was to do. It's who I am and who I've always been.

HOW CAN THEY HEAR,
UNLESS THEY HAVE A PREACHER?

I mentioned this briefly in an earlier chapter, but in my teens and 20s, my mother constantly told me stories about me when I was 4-5 years old. She said, "We lived in Ft. Worth, Texas, on 2521 Lebow, on a corner lot. While your sisters were in school, like clockwork, you'd go outside with your little New Testament to stand on the street corner and preach. You'd preach to the dog and the person riding their bike. When the city bus would come by, you'd preach to it, and then to the cars that drove by. You would even preach when there wasn't anyone around. You'd preach for an hour or so and then come in and ask for a snack. Scott, you did that for over 2 years," she'd say. "You even always wanted to dress differently than other

---

*The purpose of the pastor is to give you something
to hear, because faith comes by hearing, so that the
power of possibility can be released into your life.*

---

boys. You wanted a suit, tie, dress pants and dress shoes, and when we could afford it, we bought those clothes for you. You preferred to wear dress clothes to school instead of school clothes, so you would."

What was I doing? Being who God had called me to be.

I was saved when I was 3, led to Jesus by my Sunday school teacher, a little petite French woman whose name was Audienne Brochire. She was a quiet, very mild-mannered, but very powerful woman, who carried the presence of Jesus. Her sidekick was a white-haired woman named Mary Greg. Mary was the opposite of Audienne. She was a short, fiery preacher with a gruff voice, who absolutely would put the fear of God in you. At that time, my mother had been saved and grown into a powerful intercessor. Dad wasn't born again yet, not until I was 7, but it didn't seem to matter to Mom because every Sunday morning without fail, she would rise early, get us four children up, make breakfast, get us all dressed and take us to church. Even then as a kid, I was completely engrossed in the preacher. I hung on every word—even words I couldn't understand. I studied the preacher's actions, how he carried himself, his voice… everything. Intuitively, I knew somehow that's who I was.

It wasn't until I was in my middle teens, after my mom had prayed my dad into the kingdom—along with all of his sisters and brothers and their kids—did I realize that I was born to be a preacher. I didn't set out to learn to be one, I just knew it was my purpose. In fact, when I was 13, I was sitting in a meeting with my family, preparing for the service that would begin in 10 minutes…when a voice spoke so loud to me on the inside that it seemed very real and audible.

- *You will work for a preacher who will touch the world*
- *You will sing for a global ministry that will impact the world mightily*
- *You will have a powerful ministry one day*

I wrote all three of these in my Bible. Those three directives became the three landmarks of my life that have guided my journey. As I'm writing this book, the first two have come to pass, and I'm living in the building process of the third.

As I've said, at 39, I started BelieversWay Ministries and planted our first church. Most ministers feel called to start their ministries much earlier, but God didn't direct me that way. One day, I asked the Lord, "What took you so long?"

He answered, "Jesus didn't begin his earthly ministry until he was 30, and he was the Son of God. Who do you think you are?"

121

Good point!

Preachers have forever shaped my life. I have such a love, compassion and understanding of them. They move me, because I know what they are born to do. I understand personally that it's not optional to fulfill your calling as a minister, not if you want to live at peace with yourself. Unlike many occupations that are easily changed, God

> *Everyone needs a preacher in his or her life. It's one of God's strategies for you to hear directives and experience the power of possibility in your life.*

doesn't give preachers a choice. The Bible makes it clear: "The gifts and callings of God are without repentance."[1] You may feel that way about your occupation as well, that God ordained for you to do it from the time you were a child. If so, then you understand some of what I'm describing. Preachers have an assignment on their lives, an anointing, a drive that is so uncommon, they stand out like a sore thumb in the crowd. I love what I do and that God has called me to do it. I can't imagine doing anything else.

Preachers—those who have authentically responded to the call of God, who are willing to lay down their lives for God's people— are as rare and unusual as Elijah, John the Baptist and Paul. There's a reason for that. Paul writes, "For whoever calls on the name of the Lord shall be saved. How then shall they call on Him in whom they have not believed? And how shall they believe in Him of whom they have not heard? And how shall they hear without a preacher?"[2]

Everyone needs a preacher in his or her life. It's one of God's strategies for you to hear directives and experience the power of possibility in your life.

GOD WANTS YOU TO GET IT!

Preachers are all throughout the Bible—and all the way through history to our present day. They've been called different names, but they are all messengers from God with a message for God's people.

In the Old Testament, according to biblical history after Moses died, the leadership baton was passed from Moses to Joshua, and it was Joshua's job to take God's people over the Jordan River into the Promised Land. Moses was their preacher first, and now it was Joshua. He was the spokesperson through whom God would now speak and give direction to the people.

As they entered the Promised Land, the first city God's people came to was a fortified city called Jericho.[3] It was walled and filled with thousand of enemies. (It's just like God to call a man into the ministry to pastor and tell him immediately go to battle for a city, community or country!) The people who lived there thought the land was theirs and rightfully so because they had built the city. They had no intentions of just handing over the territory to God's children because they occupied the land.

> *God's ways are different than ours, which means He probably will either solve it in a way that doesn't make sense to us, or have us do something in a way that seems unreasonable, or even impossible. Either way, it will make faith! It will ignite the power of possibility.*

But God had told Joshua to enter and possess the land, so it had to be accomplished. Joshua knew the power of possibility. He knew God was the God of impossibilities, so he went to Him and said, "Lord, here we are. What are you going to do about our enemies?

They have a fortified city, and we don't have the necessary weapons to bring these people down."

God had a plan, as Joshua knew He would. The Lord told Joshua to get up the next morning and preach to the people. Yes, believe it or not, God's answer was for Joshua to preach. Why? Because people need a preacher to know what to do. How will they hear, unless they have a preacher?[4]

The Lord told Joshua to tell them that they were going to march around the city one time, but they weren't to make any noise.

Hmmm. That's different. What good is that going to do? But they did it anyway.

Joshua preached, and then they went out and marched, even though it didn't make any sense. Do you know what happened? Nothing.

I have found in my experiences, that there are two things we must understand when we go to God for direction:

1. If our problem doesn't make sense, why do we assume God will give us an answer that does?
2. While God always hears our prayers and always answers them, He doesn't always do something immediately.

God's ways are different than ours, which means He probably will either solve it in a way that doesn't make sense to us, or have us do something in a way that seems unreasonable, or even impossible. Either way, it will make faith! It will ignite the power of possibility.

Even though Joshua didn't understand why they marched, and then nothing happened, He had faith in God's plan, so He prayed and talked to God again. The Lord told Him to get up the next morning, preach the same message and do the same thing. So Joshua preached. It didn't make sense…but that didn't matter.

Now at this point, after the people heard they were going to do the same thing that seemingly got them nowhere the day before, you know some of them had to be thinking, *This doesn't make sense—we should do something different because that didn't work yesterday.*

They were at a decision point—trust their own logic or trust the Word of God that came from the preacher. Did God really tell him to tell us to do that? How many times have you questioned the preacher?

When those doubts arise, you have to make a choice. Trust what God has spoken or not.

These people had seen God do the impossible in some really strange ways many times before, so they chose to trust the preacher. They marched again quietly around the city. And nothing happened—again.

Whenever a leader—or preacher—possesses a voice of value, it becomes a place not only of influence, but also of power, demonstration and full expression.

Each day, the preacher preached the same message. The people acted in response to the message and nothing happened. *Are you sure God told this preacher to minister this specific word to us?*

The next morning, God said to preach the same message, do the same march, and they got the same result—nothing. This went on for six days.

Imagine what these people's minds must have been telling them: *This is pointless! We have done what this preacher told us to do for nearly a week now and nothing has happened! Why are we doing it again?*

Does this sound familiar? Has this ever happened to you when the preacher gave you a word from God? Did you quit after a few days, a few weeks, or a few months because you didn't think it was working? I believe this story is simply a snapshot of your personal journey with the preacher God has supernaturally called you to connect with—and it's encouragement to choose to trust.

The children of Israel had faith in the plan God gave them through the minister who preached to them. It's interesting God calls them children. In my experience, children by nature and development are immature. They whine, fuss, and are determined not to do what they are told. They always have a better way and think they know more than the parent, but not these children. We don't hear that the children of Israel complained or griped about the message or what the preacher told them to do. I believe it's because they truly believed their preacher and that God had given him the plan.

Joshua's voice had value with the children of Israel. Certainly this speaks to his lifestyle, his example, his leadership abilities and skills, but it also speaks of his congregation. Whenever a leader—or preacher—possesses a voice of value, it becomes a place not only of

When our faith answers the call to action, it creates life.

influence, but also of power, demonstration and full expression. That person can totally be himself. This creates an atmosphere of expectation and anticipation. He has the "ear" of his congregation. They trust him.

So, in Joshua's case, the congregation had faith and the preacher had faith. Even today, this ideal interaction creates a corporate action that causes the enemy's strongholds to come down in the people's lives. When people put action to the direction the preacher gives, it produces results. James tells us, "Faith without works is dead."[5] When our faith answers the call to action, it creates life. It creates an environment where awesome things happen.

The preacher is important to God...because you are important to God. The preacher is one of His strategies to get answers to you, directions to you, encouragement to you, so the power of possibility can be working in your life.

The Message expresses this well: "But God's not finished. He's waiting around to be gracious to you. He's gathering strength to show mercy to you. God takes the time to do everything right—everything. Those who wait around for Him are the lucky ones. Oh yes, people of Zion, citizens of Jerusalem, your time of tears is over. Cry for help and you'll find its grace and more grace. The moment He hears, He'll answer. Just as the Master kept you alive during the hard times, he'll keep your teacher [preacher] alive and present among you. Your teacher [preacher] will be right there, local and on the job, urging you on whenever you wander left or right."[6]

At times, Jesus preached to congregations where His voice had value. Other times, the people judged His words as not important. Matthew records that "Jesus went to his own hometown and could do no mighty work because of their unbelief."[7] To those people in Nazareth, His voice had no value. People there could have been healed, delivered or saved, but because they didn't value Jesus' voice, they didn't get the answers for which they were probably crying out to God.

How blessed for the children of Israel that they valued Pastor Joshua's words. How blessed for them that they valued his direction—which was God's direction.

Because of their faith—and Joshua's faith—every morning they did what Joshua had told them to do. March...quietly and return to camp. God had them repeat the process six times with no results—or so it looked—but God always has a purpose for repeating Himself.

For example, have you ever noticed that the Bible says the same things over and over, just in different ways? Think about Matthew,

Mark, Luke and John—they are all the story of Jesus' life and ministry on earth, just told in different ways. All are the same story with a different perspective.

Why would God repeat Jesus' life story four times? Because He wants us to get it! And He wanted the children of Israel to understand that the upcoming victory at Jericho had nothing to do with them or their thoughts and plans. He wanted them to be very clear

---

God's ways are different than ours but they always make faith. They always open up our lives to the power of possibility.

---

on whose idea it was—after all, what man would come up with a plan like this one? The victory seemed impossible. The instructions for victory didn't make sense. Sounds like a setup for the power of possibility to work!

On the sixth night, the Lord said to do the same thing, but change it up just a little. This time they were to march around the city six times quietly and then on the seventh time around, the priest was to blow the trumpet, the people were to shout and praise the Lord, and then they were to break clay pots.

Now, if marching silently didn't make sense, this surely didn't either! But let's keep following the story…and see all the faith it made!

God's instructions didn't say on the third time, or the fourth go around to shout, praise and break pots. No, He said to wait until the seventh time.

So around they went, once, twice, three times—not making a sound. Four, five, six times—still quiet, but on the seventh time, the priest blew the trumpet resounding the declaration of victory for all to hear, then God's people shouted giving praise to the Lord and clay pots were crushed—and the walls came tumbling down!

"So every man charged straight in, and they took the city. They devoted the city to the Lord and destroyed with the sword every living thing in it—men and women, young and old, cattle, sheep and donkeys."[8]

The enemy was crushed, but there were no casualties in this war. Why? Because they did it God's way.

But it just doesn't make sense! It wasn't designed to make sense—it was designed to create faith. It was designed for them to experience the power of possibility.

God told Joshua—the preacher—the war strategies that He wanted to use to defeat the enemy. It was Joshua's responsibility to take the message back to the people. The plan didn't make sense to the natural mind, not even to the intellect of Joshua. But he preached the message God told him to preach anyway. It seemed impossible to the people that this would actually make a difference, but they did it and crossed over into another dimension in faith, releasing the power of possibility into their circumstance.

God is determined to get you to your destiny.

For us to live in that kind of victory, we have to quit living on the level of our natural intelligence, where our own thoughts and ways determine every move and define our very existence. We have to start living in a non-linear dimension of faith where the power of possibility is accessed. But let me warn you now, Joshua is not the only preacher God told to do things that people's minds just didn't understand. Many preachers have followed in his footsteps over hundreds of years. Thank God they have! Because of their boldness, answers have come to believing congregations.

God's ways are different than ours. There are a lot of things that He says that just don't make any sense at all, and those things confound our reasoning at times and leave many of us looking perplexed, like a deer in the headlights. His ways are so far above our own thinking, but they always make faith. They always open up our lives to the power of possibility.

As a preacher, I've boldly declared what God has told me to tell His people. I've preached to them good news that challenged them to change, to grow, to move forward, all because the answers they were asking for were in their responses to the messages I preached. In other words, as they took to heart what I was saying, God revealed Himself to them. God gave them answers. They experienced the power of possibility.

I've taught on our television program—*BelieversWay With Scott and Missy,* **www.believersway.tv**—revelation about relationships—messages from the preacher—that God wants His people to receive and thrive in. God is determined to get you to your destiny. He's determined to get you the answers and direction you need—and one of His strategies is to use the preacher.

> *I watched as my dad and mom did some unusual things—things that didn't make sense, but always made faith, things that always opened the door for the power of possibility.*

That's how believers are saved. "How then will they call on Him in whom they have not believed? How will they believe in Him whom they have not heard? And how will they hear without a preacher?"[9] Someone preached the gospel to you, and you responded. Someone is still preaching the gospel to you. Are you still responding?

THE PATIENCE OF A PREACHER

My dad responded—finally. After my mom prayed him into the kingdom, he became a preacher. Mom prayed so much, all of Dad's family became Christians, and many of them went on to become preachers as well. I come from a great legacy of faith.

Growing up, I watched as my dad and mom did some unusual things—things that didn't make sense, but always made faith, things that always opened the door for the power of possibility.

When I was 7 years old, I remember a man who came to our door in the middle of the night. (People came to our door a lot!) It was before my dad was saved, and the man was a preacher who came calling on my dad. God had told him to tell Dad about Christ.

"Where's Kenneth Johnson?" he asked Mom when she opened the door.

"He's not home yet. I'm sure he's out gambling," she told him.

It was Friday night and payday was always on a Friday. Dad would gamble his paycheck away and then take his frustration out on Mom and us kids.

"Do you mind, Joyce, if I sit out here on the porch until he comes home?"

"No, you can sit out here all night if you want to. I'm going to bed."

Mom locked the door and turned off the porch light. Sometime after midnight, Dad showed up. There was the preacher patiently waiting on him. Together they talked about the things of God until the sun came up Saturday morning and Dad surrendered his life to Jesus. How could he have heard without a preacher?

What happened changed everything. The next morning was Sunday—and it was very different than any other Sunday in my life up to that point. Dad got up, put his suit on and went to church with us. It was the answer to years of my mom's fervent prayers.

In the church service, Dad publicly professed Jesus as his Lord and Savior. From that day forward he got very involved in the church, and started helping in "Royal Rangers"—the outreach program of the children's ministry to teach boys and girls the message of the gospel. Eighteen months later he began helping in the prayer ministry, which was a part of our church's men's ministry. He did all this while working his Monday through Friday job at the Fort Worth Star-Telegram newspaper. During this time he also took the famous Dale Carnegie® course that taught him confidence in public speaking and interacting with others.

It was during this season of his life that people began to gather around him, and he recognized that he had an anointing and an influence. He recognized that everything he did or led in the church grew. People were attracted to him. The pastor recognized this too and asked him to be over the men's group—so Dad taught the men in the church.

Long story short, by the time I was 8 or so, Dad recognized that he was called to the ministry.

Soon, Dad pastored a little church in Spearman, Texas, with a congregation of almost 100 people for about two years. Then, he believed God was calling us to the mission field—so we moved to Oklahoma (LOL). He took a pastoral position at another small church there for several years.

This all occurred in the mid 70s, and the United States was in a deep recession. The engines that drove the community where we lived were agriculture, cattle, gas wells, oil money, and a community of about 8,000 people. Needless to say, there wasn't much tithe and offerings coming into this little church.

SOW A CAR...

But it didn't faze Dad. At one point, he was in a series of sermons preaching on faith. The more he preached on it, the bolder he got and the stronger he grew. (You can see faith and hear faith. You know when someone understands it, and when they don't—and it was all over Dad! He understood it!)

About the fourth Sunday into the series of messages, my dad just said something that came straight up out of his heart. It was full of faith: "If God told me to give my only car away, I would give it away right now, because I have faith and I believe in Him and in fact, I'm giving it to you." He gave the car to Faith, an unmarried, middle-aged woman in the church who had no family.

Well, this wasn't the first time my daddy had given away a car. I'd watched him years earlier give a car away to a teenager—the only car our family owned. That teenager was my cousin, Willie George, who now pastors Church on the Move in Tulsa, Okla. (He was more fruit of Mom's praying Dad's brothers and sisters into the kingdom). So it didn't surprise me that now he was giving away a second car.

You can see faith and hear faith.

That put us on foot again, right? Almost. There was a man who owned a used car dealership in that little town who heard what my dad did. He called and said, "Hey, I'll let you borrow one of our vehicles. Just drive it." I think he felt sorry for us.

Months later, as was our family custom in those days, we went to Tulsa, to Kenneth E. Hagin's camp meeting. (Camp Meeting was their name for a week-long meeting of church services.) In the first session of the first day of that camp meeting, Kenneth Hagin said to a crowd of about 500-600 people, "Kenneth Johnson, the Lord's told me..." and he did the very same thing that my dad had done back in our little church! He gave us a car—a new car that the ministry had bought two weeks earlier. After the service, he also wrote a check, gave it to Mom and Dad, filled the back of that station wagon—which was equivalent to the same capacity of a large SUV today—with hundreds of his books, and said, "Now, wherever you go, I want you to sell these books and put the proceeds into your ministry."

Never underestimate the power God intended for your life with the strategy of having you receive from a preacher.

My dad understood faith! He recognized that in a time of recession, it's not the time to withhold. It's not the time to get stingy. It's the time to sow a seed and in the same year, he received a hundredfold harvest—the same year! What did my dad do? He preached a message God told him to preach, and by faith did what God told him to do, and experienced the power of possibility. It didn't make sense in the natural at the time, but it made faith!

He gave answers as a preacher—and he received answers from a preacher. He acted in one setting as the preacher with faith...and in the next setting as the congregation member with faith. Do you see the power of corporate faith operating in the relationship God created—the one between the preacher and the people? Never underestimate the power God intended for your life with the strategy of having you receive from a preacher. It's part of God's great plan for your walking in the power of possibility.

CHAPTER 10

MAKE THE SWITCH

LEARN TO THINK GOD'S THOUGHTS

God loves you so much He wants you to live from the spiritual dimension where He is, and where everything is possible. He has called you to His ways and His thoughts, but they are on a level far above yours.

"'For my thoughts are not your thoughts, neither are your ways my ways,' declares the Lord. 'As the heavens are higher than the earth, so are my ways higher than your ways and my thoughts than your thoughts. As the rain and the snow come down from heaven, and do not return to it without watering the earth and making it bud and flourish, so that it yields seed for the sower and bread for the eater, so is my word that goes out from my mouth: It will not return to me empty, but will accomplish what I desire and achieve the purpose for which I sent it.'"[1]

So often we try to pull God down to our level, but He tells us very clearly here that His ways and thoughts are higher. He can't be pulled down—but we can ascend upward into His thoughts, ways and paths.

Our ways are not God's ways because we do not think like He does. So, if we change our thoughts to match His, we will discover new ways. But to do that, we have to open ourselves up to all the possibilities, and connect to them with our thoughts.

> *God tells us very clearly here that His ways and thoughts are higher. He can't be pulled down— but we can ascend upward into His thoughts, ways and paths.*

He told us through the Apostle Paul: "Do not conform any longer to the pattern of this world, but be transformed by the renewing of your mind. Then you will be able to test and approve what God's will is—His good, pleasing and perfect will."[2] So, we must train our minds how to think the thoughts of God, and then we will know God's ways and His perfect will.

God knows His thoughts and ways are so much higher than our own, so He gave us the tools we would need to renew our minds and come up to a higher way of thinking and doing—to the ways that seem impossible and don't always make sense.

Before you had a relationship with God, through Jesus Christ, you lived your life on one level. It was your personal life. It consisted of "self this" and "self that." It was full of self-evaluation, self-helps, self-worth, selfish motives, self-esteem and selfish ambition. But after you were born again, you began living on two levels.

Level A: Your personal life.

Level B: Your life inside the kingdom of God.

This is why you started pursuing God, going to church, reading Christian books, watching Christian shows like BelieversWay TV, reading your Bible, attending a small group, and other special meetings. You wanted what Jesus instructed us to do in His life-shaping statement: "Seek first the Kingdom of God and His righteousness and all these things will be added unto you."[3]

This statement changed everything for you. Jesus was literally challenging you to make the switch in your priorities—putting "B" as "A," and "A" as "B."

So it looks like this.

Level A: Your life inside the kingdom.

Level B: Your personal life.

When you make "the switch," your personal life is finally impacted by the kingdom of God, and all "these things" are added unto you.

When you make "the switch," God begins speaking to you about "you." He gets specific, and you get clarity about who you are in the kingdom, your office, gifting, callings, anointing and assignments because "the gifts and callings of God are without repentance."[4]

If we change our thoughts to match God's, we will discover new ways.

As a preacher, I am accountable to God for my gifts and callings—but so are you. We all have callings—whether in the marketplace or in the Church.

As a priest—that's what the Bible calls a preacher as well—I'm responsible to give vision, timing, direction, and the blessing. These are the four elements of life about which that I'm called to assist the believer. Of these four, my primary responsibility as a priest is to give people vision for their lives.

Why vision? Well, in part because of what the Word says about it. "Where there is no progressive vision, the people perish."[5]

Many people don't recognize the power of vision. Vision has powerful capacity. Notice this verse doesn't say, "Where there is no progressive vision, the individual perishes. The person perishes. The individual family perishes."

No, there is a vastness to this power. It is "the people—God's people—who perish."

We are supposed to run to WIN!

Other translations like the *Free Berean Bible* and the *American Baptist Publishing Society* say it even more insightfully:

"Where there is no progressive vision, people run wild. The people are unrestrained."

"Where there is progressive vision, God's people stay in their lane. God's people keep their life on God's course."

Why is that important for me to stay in my lane, to stay on course?

Well, first of all Paul said, "We as believers are running a race," and we are supposed to run that race to lose.[6]

Not hardly. I can't imagine any runners running to lose. No, runners run to win. They're competitors. If you're an athlete, you do it to win. You don't like to lose, and if you're a really competitive athlete, you're probably a sore loser!

We are not supposed to run in our Christian experience just to barely make it to the finish line, dive for the tape and yell: "I MADE IT!"

No, we are supposed to run to WIN! To do that you will have to cast off every weight and every sin that so easily besets you—the ones that are slowing you down.[7] You are to win the race that's set before you, and you can do that because you have vision. It's the force of vision that keeps you on course.

What gets you off course? Storms—financial storms, physical storms, relational storms. James tells us, "But let him ask in faith, nothing wavering. For he that wavereth is like a wave of the sea driven with the wind and tossed."[8]

What happens if we have no vision and the trouble comes? It blows us off the path. A believer who is possessed and obsessed by God's vision in the kingdom of God won't be blown off course. He will stay in his lane, run his race and grab the prize.

Jesus warned us: "For everyone who comes to Me and listens to My words [in order to heed their teaching] and does them, I will show you what he is like: He is like a man building a house, who dug and went down deep and laid a foundation upon the rock; and when a flood arose, the torrent broke against that house and could not shake or move it, because it had been securely built or founded on a rock. But he who merely hears and does not practice doing My words is like a man who built a house on the ground without a foundation, against which the torrent burst, and immediately it collapsed and fell, and the breaking and ruin of that house was great."[9]

A believer who is possessed and obsessed by God's vision in the kingdom of God won't be blown off course.

Even as a believer, you can have all the provision in the world, but if you don't have a preacher speaking the vision of God in your life, you're going to live unrestrained, even wild like an untamed animal.

Just watch *E! News* or pick up a *People Magazine* or a *Sports Illustrated*. You'll read about a basketball player or a football player whose making $25 million dollars to play a kid's game. You'll read how he's been found in a hotel room with prostitutes and cocaine on the table. What's wrong with this guy? He doesn't have a preacher speaking the vision of God into his life.

God desires to ignite in you whom He created you to be, and only then will the power of possibility become reality in your life. When this happens, you'll think the thoughts of God, and then God will give you new thoughts. You'll have dreams of being the head and not the tail. You'll have visions of being above and not beneath, so

> *God desires to ignite in you whom He created you to be, and only then will the power of possibility become reality in your life.*

you'll prosper and not retreat. You'll be first instead of last. This will allow you to go forward and never fail. You'll be favored by God and man, and excel in your job. You'll possibly start your own business. Your life will take a turn—not for the worse—but for the better. And you'll begin doing incredible things for the kingdom of God, and the kingdom of God will bring incredible things into your life…all because you made "the switch" from living in your own reasoning to living in His thoughts and ways.

CHAPTER 11

EXPRESS YOUR FAITH

AND MAKE IT GROW

One morning as I was in my office preparing for a new series of messages, a strong spirit of faith came on me. I began declaring, decreeing and speaking the Word.

The Holy Spirit led me to walk out into the hall and pass the doorway to the team room where our staff was engaged in a meeting. I leaned into the room and asked: "Hey, who in here needs a car—and I mean really needs a car—because the one you have is in bad shape?"

Two men raised their hands. I began prophesying over their lives, finances and vehicles. I ended declaring, "Your cars are coming now in Jesus' Name!"

Within 12 months of my making that declaration, both of these men were given cars. They didn't go buy cars—they were given cars within ten days of each other!

The power of possibility is available when we begin expressing our faith! I'm not telling you this story to impress you. I am as normal a believer as you are, but I'm one who expresses my faith. I'm telling you this story because this power of possibility is available to you just as it was to me. The greater one lives in both of us.[1] Jesus said we'd do greater works, actions and deeds, that produce awesome results, that even supersede His. We are supposed to live this way—

Our journey with God through Jesus Christ starts in a familiar place. It begins with trust and faith.

declaring and decreeing things that need to be. We're to express our faith, because when we do, it grows!

God is waiting with baited breath for you—the believer—to begin tackling the tough issues of life by simply expressing your faith—publicly!

WE GROW UP IN IT

Our journey with God through Jesus Christ starts in a familiar place. One that is not so unique and far removed from the norm. It begins with trust and faith. Just as you were born into a family that you did not choose, a genetic coding was purposefully designed and assigned to you. You were under the care of a mother and father who nurtured, raised and trained you. They met your physical, emotional, intellectual and soul needs. At one time you were totally dependent on the love and mercy of others. So you naturally trusted. You naturally had faith in them.

It's the same way in our walk with God. Your relationship with Him is formed out of a similar bond. When you were born again, you first confessed with your mouth and believed with faith in your heart.[2] Your relationship began with faith and trust—and it is through faith that you will continue to thrive, grow and expand!

When you were a baby, you had no choice whether to trust those entrusted with your care. Today, as an adult, you have a choice.

In your relationship with God, you trusted easily when you were first born again. Today, you have to choose. Your relationship with Him can grow beyond obedience to friendship, from servant hood to royal respect. But first, like a child under the direction of a parent, you obey without understanding the reasons why. Then as relational growth occurs through consistency, and as your mind is renewed, you move and are promoted from a childlike relationship to an adult relationship with God.

There will always be people and circumstances to discourage you, to try and stop you from growing, but you have the power to fight that.

God is so into relationship. I believe it was one of his best ideas, and as it continues, there's an ongoing development that takes place within you and between you and God. As you journey together, other ways of relating are introduced through mutual respect and interaction, where explanation produces understanding. As you journey living a life of faith in consistent interaction with God and His Word, understanding accumulates in your heart and mind. You gain wisdom and your faith increases.

YOU DON'T NEED A FRIENEMY

Let's kick the can a little further down the road. I know this is deep, but it's the understanding you desire and need. God wants you to grow, thrive and expand in your faith. He wants you to express it, live it and mature in it. That's actually how it grows! By using it.

There will always be people and circumstances to discourage you, to try and stop you from growing, but you have the power to fight that. You can walk in wisdom and protect your airspace, your environment and your friendships. God wants you in the right relationships to help you grow.

For example, I've never met anyone who can live with a nag. You can't move forward or enjoy life with someone who constantly points out your mistakes, failures or sins every day. I've never been able to make friends with people who were continuously pointing

---

God wants us to make our past pay for our future—not be a place where we live.

---

out my missed steps. I can't be friends with people who are talking behind my back, defriending me on social network sites, and playing games that hurt me and other people. No one really can! We all have weaknesses—those things that potentially produce setbacks, and occasional failures in our lives. Have you ever had an experience where a close friend turned hostile and became a rogue enemy—a frienemy? It is so painful!

In truth, we are drawn to people who see our value and strength, who see the best in us, who value and admire our best characteristics. When there is someone in your life who says:
- "Remember what you did…"
- "You're not good enough…"
- "They'll never like you…"
- "That can't happen for you…"
- "You made this mistake or that mistake…"

…they are an accuser—someone who is judgmental and a nag—someone who maximizes our faults and eliminates even the memory of our strengths.

Missy and I have three sons. From eldest to youngest, they are seven years apart. As I've watched each of their journeys, it seems as if they have to go through the same negative experiences over and over again before they finally realize, "You know, I ought to stop doing that."

Their cycles of discovery and revelation have taught me things about my life and people in general. Our journeys are not exactly the same, but our landmarks—those places we all have to pass—are very similar. In other words, we all have to learn the same lessons—we're just different kinds of students!

In our immaturity, many times we have to learn the lesson about a situation more than once or twice—and sometimes dozens of times. We repeat mistakes going around the same mountain again and again. But as we get older and become more mature, we go through something once and say to ourselves things like:

> *God doesn't see us through the filter of our flaws. He views us through the filter of His Word. God never judges us, and He doesn't accuse or nag either.*

"I'm never going through that again."
"It was too painful."
"That was too high of a price to pay."
"Stupid, stupid, stupid."

The point is we learned and grew from the experience, so then we qualify to move up into new levels of life. God wants us to make our past pay for our future—not be a place where we live. Our past is to pay for our dreams, and be fuel for the journey ahead.

God doesn't see us through the filter of our flaws. He views us through the filter of His Word. God never judges us, and He doesn't accuse or nag either.

The Word says, "Then I heard a loud voice shouting across the heavens, 'It has come at last—salvation and power and the Kingdom of our God, and the authority of his Christ. For the accuser of our brothers and sisters has been thrown down to earth—the one who accuses them [which is us] before our God day and night.'"[3]

The accuser is never God. It is never the Holy Spirit. The accuser is the devil. He is the one who accuses, condemns, and judges us as guilty—and sadly, he uses people to facilitate his purpose. In other words, he influences others to speak the accusations, condemnation and guilt.

One of my favorite verses helps me stand in faith when the accusations are flying: "No weapon formed against you shall prosper, and every tongue which rises against you in judgment you shall condemn. This is the heritage of the servants of the Lord, and their righteousness is from Me."[4]

What kind of tongue? An accusing tongue—a voice that speaks accusations, points the finger, looks down its nose, and judges. It's the enemy—the devil—who finds volunteers to do his work. Through others, he assaults using words against us.

THE ASSASSINATION ATTEMPT

Relationships can either be a powerful tool or a vicious weapon. (I'm speaking from the pain of experience.) I've learned so much, and accepted so much, all to constructively build a life that continues to be sensitive to God. It's the enemy who is trying to hinder our growth. God wants us to live free and unhurt, always sensitive to Him and His leading. To live as God wants, I've had to learn some lessons that can help you as well.

First, refuse to change who God has hardwired you to be in order to become who people want you to be. Jesus demonstrated this for us in His life so we could imitate His example.

One day in Nazareth, after Jesus preached His first message on the anointing, the crowd rose up against Him. They drove Him out of town and took Him to the brow of the hill, on which the town was built, in order to throw Him off the cliff.[5] It was an assassination attempt!

I admire Jesus for not quitting after this failed attempt on His life. I equally honor Him for continuing to be who God had hardwired Him to be without any apology. It was His first message and

> *God wants us to thrive and grow in our faith and relationship with Him.*

they tried to kill Him! By any standard, this was not a good day!

After His very first message, He not only wrestled with accusations and finger pointing, He had to face a potential assassination. I've had some tough days in ministry but never that bad!

We all have to learn how to deal with rejection in a healthy way that makes us keep going—and never quit. We have to deal with rejection in a way that doesn't shut us down. We can never let what someone says or does stop us from being who God hardwired us to be.

Be Who God Hardwired You to Be

After this first message, Jesus' life in ministry could have seemed like it just wasn't meant to be. But He lived in relational trust with God—so He pressed on.

As the story continues, He left Nazareth and ministered in Capernaum, with a completely different result. His message impacted lives. The power of possibility was released into people who were healed, and at the end of His stay there, Luke's version of the story says, "At daybreak, Jesus went out to a solitary place. The people were looking for him, and when they came to where he was, they tried to keep him from leaving them."[6]

In every relational challenge there will always be either a blessing or a curse. Our response to that is what sets our course and future success.

In His first meeting, Jesus was rejected and despised. In His second, He was a star who was celebrated. The crowds pursued Him everywhere He went. But in both situations, He continued to be who God hardwired Him to be. That is how God wants us to live. It's how He wants us to thrive and grow in our faith and relationship with Him.

Jesus' strength to continue after being rejected impresses me. Equally, His fortitude to not camp out on people's adoration of Him amazes me even more. He didn't let the pain of rejection shut His identity down, and He didn't let their approval move Him into pride and arrogance. He stayed true to who God had purposely created Him to be!

No one likes rejection or disapproval. We all want to fit in, to be accepted, appreciated and loved. In every relational challenge there will always be either a blessing or a curse. Our response to that is what sets our course and future success.

It takes the God kind of faith to be who God has called you to be and to do what God has called you to do. It is inevitable in your journey that you will encounter these two types of people. Therefore, the goal is for you to have unmovable faith when you're rejected, as well as unshakable faith when you're accepted. When I'm rejected, I don't try to please those people. I don't try to win them over. I am not called to the ministry of convincing. No, God told me, "I've called you to a ministry of words. And the power of possibility is in them."

So I don't try to convince people that they've got it all wrong. I often say, "To know me is to love me." I am a good person, and I have their best interest at heart. But I can't make them understand or hear me as I mean to be heard.

No, if they don't accept me, I just move on. If I don't—and if you don't—then the very people who resist us will eventually paralyze us, and we will start projecting insecurity and fear. As a preacher, that would cause me to minister God's truths through a filter of hurt and pain, which would lead to a skewed message. For you, it would cause you to interact with your family and friends through a filter of hurt and pain that would skew your perspectives. Your jaded interpretation of life and situations would cause you to draw incorrect conclusions every day.

It takes the God kind of faith to be who God has called you to be and to do what God has called you to do.

Let me illustrate this further. Have you ever met an angry Christian—someone who's all fired up about something they think is a righteous cause? They are angry because they wrongly think God is angry with them.

Judgmental believers have the same problem. They think God is judging them, so they judge others.

How many born again children of God do you know who condemn their fellow believers? They do that because they think God is condemning them.

This is not what the Word says. God lovingly told us through the Apostle Paul "God is for you, not against you."[7]

When you know God is for you, you're for people, regardless of where they are in their journey. You don't care how mature or immature they are. You don't care how imperfect they are. You understand that some people are at the beginning of their journey, others are a quarter of the way, others are half way, and others are even farther along the path.

We are to grow upward into Christ Jesus.[8] As believers we must allow each other space to do that. All believers are at different levels of faith and experience in their relationship with God.

When we live liberated through who we are in Christ Jesus, we live with a sin-free mindset—a guilt-free consciousness. Living free of guilt allows us to no longer judge and condemn others, as well as ourselves.

I decided years ago, no matter where you are at in your pursuit of God, I'm with you and for you every step of the way. I am without judgment concerning any area of your life. I am without accusation or condemnation.

I've known the Holy Spirit for more than 40 years now. He doesn't convict me of sin. He doesn't remind me of my failure and mistakes. He always speaks to me of my righteousness in Christ Jesus. He always talks to me from my future—telling me what I can be in God, what I can do in God, who I am hardwired to be. He's for me and not against me!

Jesus set the standard high, which is why we are to continually look to Him because He is the one who authors and finishes our journey of faith.[9] Discover this truth—God's truth—about who you are: "There is now no condemnation for those who are in Christ Jesus."[10] This is really you!

There is absolutely "no condemnation" for us as believers. So our adversary's only weapon is a condemning tongue. When we live liberated through who we are in Christ Jesus, we live with a sin-free mindset—a guilt-free consciousness. Living free of guilt allows us to no longer judge and condemn others, as well as ourselves.

In truth, we are drawn to those people who see value in us, who consider us worthwhile. They see our strengths and look beyond our faults. They see the best in us and believe the best of us. That's how God sees you. God is on your side. He sees His greatness in you. After all, you were worth the very blood of His only beloved son. You are worthy.

This type of nonjudgmental acceptance seems impossible to the un-renewed mind, but you have the mind of Christ.[11] It perplexes the intellect of the religious. To them it doesn't make sense, but God believes in Jesus, and you are in Him! Settle it and say it: God accepts me!

Now, on our quest, there will be things, situations, circumstances, problems and dilemmas that seem impossible. Many of those things do not make sense, so God will give you an answer that doesn't make sense either. He will require you to do something that, to the natural mind, doesn't seem feasible, practical or even reasonable. Will you believe Him as He believes in you?

Living by faith makes you pliable, bendable, flexible, even bouncy. Yes, unbreakable.

Yes, your problem came from a dimension of unreasonableness, which is why God, from the same dimension will potentially bring you an impractical application that will produce a supernatural result. Encoded in the DNA of your word from God is the power of possibility. The expression of your faith activates it.

The Apostle Paul explained to us: "For our light and momentary troubles are achieving for us an eternal glory that far outweighs them all. So we fix our eyes not on what is seen, but on what is unseen. For what is seen is temporary, but what is unseen is eternal."[12] In these verses, God is distinguishing two ways people live. Some live by what they see—the facts or the visible reality—and that determines their beliefs. Others live by faith—an invisible reality—and that determines their beliefs.

God sees us through the filter of His words, not through the perspective of our circumstances.

Living by only what you can see makes you rigid, stiff, hard, crusty, inflexible and breakable. It causes you to put your trust in only what you know and can feel. You can imagine what this produces in your life.

Living by faith makes you pliable, bendable, flexible, even bouncy. Yes, unbreakable. It results from putting your trust in God—and His greatness. You can also imagine the success that this can create.

So which one are you? Breakable...or unbreakable? Which one describes you the most? Because God sees us as the latter.

God sees us through the filter of His words, not through the perspective of our circumstances. As He speaks to us, faith rises up in us—our redeemed nature emerges from within us.

And when we express it, it grows and grows.

CHAPTER 12

TRUST GOD—NO MATTER WHAT

AND HE WILL HONOR YOUR FAITH

God has called believers to a life of faith. My faith is built on what I know—just as yours should be:

I know God is good.

I know God is faithful.

I know God is for me, and not against me.

I know God loves me.

I know God is thinking about me!

I know God has a plan for my life!

As a believer this is my source of faith! It's what makes me flexible to this seen reality. "Faith comes by hearing and hearing the Word of God."[1] The more of the Word of God I hear, the more flexible, pliable, bendable, and unbreakable I become. This is why God invented tools to help us like church, pastors, and the Bible. These tools inspire us and get to us the source of faith that makes us what I like to call bouncy.

When a problem arises in our lives is when our faith is revealed. Sure, we may face feelings of insecurity and uncertainty. And as people we want to understand everything. There's nothing wrong in that. But when we focus our attention and energy on comprehending and trying to figure out why, instead of using our faith in God, then we are missing the point.

Jesus was of quick understanding because He didn't judge by what He saw or heard. He only judged by what God showed Him.

If we're like the first group I mentioned in the last chapter, who live by their visible reality, then we become rigid and inflexible, ultimately failing the challenge to our faith. But as we choose to live by faith, even though we might deal with feelings of inferiority or inadequacies, we will maintain our trust in God. Maintaining our trust in God allows us to maintain our elasticity. In those seasons we become "Teflon® coated Christians" where none of the bad or negative situations stick to us. They just bounce right off!

"By faith. Abraham, when called to go to a place he would later receive as his inheritance, obeyed and went, even though he did not know where he was going."[2] Abraham did not know—and he still went. Faith is doing something God tells you to do even when you don't understand it. It's living by the unseen reality.

Again, like a parent-child relationship, this is how our relationship with God begins, and as it develops and matures, it changes to a more flexible, conversational dialogue between Him and us. I've learned if I'm going to go deeper with God, then I must prove myself on this level first. Even the Father of Faith—Abraham—began his relationship with God here. Why would ours be any different?

Remember, I'm not talking about performance, acting or pretending, but rather about our trust in Him—because we receive His

154

acceptance of us as one of His children. This is what kids do. They imitate: "Therefore be imitators of God as dear children."[3]

People don't understand why building our lives on the Word is important to God. Some Christians don't understand why tithing is important to God. Some people don't understand why building our marriages on God's Word is important to God. Others don't understand why raising our children in church is important to God. The Bible is full of things people are supposed to do, and because they don't understand it, they don't do it. As believers, we must do it even when we don't understand it, simply because He told us to. This is the beginning of our relational journey with God.

Abraham lived by faith, not by accumulating facts—not by what he saw, heard, or experienced. He lived by faith, doing things he didn't understand because God told him to. That's the kind of relationship God had with Abraham and God has with you and me. Subsequently, look what is said about Jesus in The Old Testament:

God wants you to have understanding—but that doesn't come from just knowing the facts and information. It comes from mixing faith and wisdom.

"And shall make Him of quick understanding, and His delight shall be in the reverential and obedient fear of the Lord. And He shall not judge by the sight of His eyes, neither decide by the hearing of His ears."[4]

Jesus was of quick understanding because He didn't judge by what He saw or heard. He only judged by what God showed Him. Consequently, He judged righteously because He lived by faith instead of by facts and information.

God wants you to have understanding—but that doesn't come from just knowing the facts and information. It comes from mixing faith and wisdom. It comes from what God says and shows you. This is where Jesus' understanding came from.

Trials are going to come. Challenges will arise. And it is faith that will see you through.

From the very first day of His life, Jesus was confronted by seemingly impossible situations. Beginning with His natural birth when King Herod ordered His murder, to 30 years later, when an angry crowd rejected His first message and wanted to assassinate Him. In these two crises, and in all the ones in between, it was faith that saved Him—either through His parents, or His own as He matured. Jesus met the challenges and resistance He encountered with faith and wisdom. He didn't withdraw and quit—and neither should we.

Trials are going to come. Challenges will arise. And it is faith that will see you through. Peter encourages us: "In this you greatly rejoice, though now for a little while you may have had to suffer grief in all kinds of trials. These have come so that your faith—of greater worth than gold, which perishes even though refined by fire—may be proved genuine and may result in praise, glory and honor when Jesus Christ is revealed."[5]

"These have come so that your faith may be proved genuine." In other words, these issues...

• Problems
• Financial challenges
• Relational hostility
• Illness
• Troubles and adversity...

…have come to prove that we walk by faith in an invisible reality instead of a faith in this visible reality. How can we know that our faith is genuine? We can know because we are adaptable, flexible, pliable, unbreakable…bouncing off obstacles, challenges and hindrances that seem impossible. We can know because as we simply express our faith, we start receiving supernatural outcomes.

IN YOUR TROUBLE IS YOUR SUCCESS

Your journey of faith is essential because your journey affects your dreams. Your relationship with God began when you were born again. From there you started a supernatural quest—a journey of discovery. It's a process that reveals who you are, and helps you evolve, develop, change and grow. Its final purpose is to reach your dreams—the ones God has birthed in you—and is dependent on you thriving in life through faith.

> *Your journey of faith is essential because your journey affects your dreams.*

Resistance—that force or pressure against you—will come. But it is what you do with it that will determine how quickly you reach your dreams. It can't keep you from realizing God's dreams for you—unless you allow it. What we all must do is learn to use resistance to keep us moving forward.

Take Nehemiah's journey for example. He was a servant to a king who sent him to rebuild the walls of Jerusalem. (The book of Nehemiah is in The Old Testament). God put him within the influence of prominence. The purpose was to be positioned and ready so God could use him to save the people. Yet, he was met with great resistance. He endured mockery, conspiracy, extortion, compromise, treachery, and slander.[6] Nehemiah's journey took him through great difficulty to build the walls of Jerusalem simultaneously. He had to fight off the enemy, so they built the wall with a hammer in one hand and a sword in the other.[7] Nehemiah overcame and built the wall in 52 days!

Joseph's journey was even more difficult. As a believer in his generation, he endured betrayal by his own family, was sold into slavery, suffered through false accusations of rape, and was thrown into prison unjustly. Nonetheless, he overcame and eventually was elevated to second in command under Pharaoh.

Daniel stood against the unjust edicts of a king, was thrown to the lions for dinner, survived and later was promoted to prominence to save a nation.

God may not deliver you from your situation, but He will keep you through it.

Our heroes we discussed earlier—Shadrach, Meshach and Abednego—made a statement to the world that has affected generations to this day: "There is only one God and only He will we worship."[8]

Notice that God didn't deliver any of these believers from their challenges. He didn't deliver Nehemiah from his assignment, Joseph from betrayal or prison, or Daniel from the lion's den. He didn't deliver the three Hebrew children from the fiery furnace. God didn't deliver any of them from their trial, but He kept them through each one. God may not deliver you from your situation, but He will keep you through it.

Many times, it's in the very circumstances we encounter on our journey that we experience God—because the expression of our faith releases the power of possibility into our lives.

The truth is, it's your journey—your course of development from one level to the next—that grows your faith. The problems, difficulties, storms and troubles are what happen along the way. God is the Alpha and Omega of your travels. You'll encounter Him as you go—as you stay in forward motion. As you move and pursue your relationship with Him, you'll discover His character and nature. You'll experience His presence and transfer your trust completely in Him. Jesus never said, "Come follow me and we will figure it out. We will see what happens."

No, He promised, "I'll make you."

Through our storms, He shapes our lives. He doesn't cause the storms, but He uses them. He takes what the devil means for harm and turns it for our good.[9]

A man once said, "Success is the greatest revenge." That's what God has on His mind: In your trouble is your success.

In the middle of our problems, we all deal with feelings of insecurity, inadequacy and uncertainty. We desire to understand everything—and there's nothing wrong with that. But if our attention is focused on comprehending the problem, instead of focused on the expressions of trusting God, our faith is unreal. Trusting God without fully understanding means our faith is genuine.

> *The expression of our faith releases the power of possibility into our lives.*

Since Peter wrote Romans 8:28, let's explore his experiences that brought him to tell us his conclusion about storms. After all, he wrote to us from his own journey: "These problems have come so that your faith may be proved genuine."[10]

One storm was literal. After a great meeting, Jesus had sent the disciples across the sea to the other side and He stayed behind to pray. Midway across, they encountered a storm. They were fearful for their lives with the lightning as a backdrop. They saw a "ghostly figure" walking on water. Jesus said, "Be not afraid, it's me."

Peter responded, "If it's you, bid me come."

Jesus said, "Come." At His word, Peter jumped out of the boat and started walking on water. He started out walking by faith in the power of Jesus' Word, but then he transferred over his faith into what he saw—and sunk. Peter believed what he saw—the waves, the wind, the storm—and he believed what he saw more than he believed Jesus. He began walking by sight—instead of faith—and began to drown. Ask yourself who or what do you believe the most? The answer is directly related to your life.

Matthew's account tells us even more: "When the disciples saw Him walking on the lake, they were terrified. 'It's a ghost,' they said, and cried out in fear. But Jesus immediately said to them: 'Take courage! It is I. Don't be afraid.'

"'Lord, if it's you,' Peter replied, 'tell me to come to you on the water.'

Trusting God without fully understanding means our faith is genuine.

"'Come,' He said. Then Peter got down out of the boat, walked on the water and came toward Jesus. But when he saw the wind, he was afraid and, beginning to sink, cried out, 'Lord, save me!'"[11]

Peter's comprehension talked him out of his genuine faith and he began to sink. "Immediately Jesus reached out His hand and caught him. 'You of little faith,' He said, 'why did you doubt?'"[12]

You know, there's a reason we are called "children of God." Like children, we have to mature and grow up into the realities of faith. Each of us has to learn to live this way in all areas of our lives.

Why do God's children—that would be us—do the same thing Peter did? Why do we doubt and lose trust in God the same way Peter did? He saw the wind and panicked. When we focus our eyes on the problem, reasoning and fear grip our hearts and rob us of the victory that's in our faith. It was this experience that contributed to Peter's statement: "These problems have come so that your faith may be proved genuine." This is the victory that overcomes the world even our faith.[13] Your expressions of faith will overcome every obstacle.

Where honor goes, life flows.

Even so, for many people today who have been brought up in an "informational mad society," it is not enough to simply "trust God," and to take Him at His word. They lack honor. And I've discovered that where honor goes, life flows. When our misgivings are bigger than our capacity to trust and obey, we look for a way out—by taking advice from people who haven't learned to walk by faith. Remember how Jesus described this kind of behavior? We become like the blind leading the blind into the ditch.[14]

Again, as we become mature believers, we are to look for reasons to hold on to God, not to let go of Him. We express our faith by standing up and being counted on through our life of commitment. As we do, we persevere, instead of calling it quits.

So if one could possibly peel away the layers of your life like an onion, each layer would consist of the faith that was created as you successfully navigated through each difficulty—by holding on to God and trusting Him. The more layers you have acquired, the more your faith has thrived, and the more flexible, unbreakable and bouncy you have become.

MY TROPHY ROOM

In my inner-world, I have a trophy room. I go into it from time to time in remembrance of all that God has done for me. I remember all the times He healed me, rescued me, delivered me, and gave me a promise and kept His word. I remember how He has met all my needs for decades now. I think of how He has protected my family, and me and kept us safe in every way. I think of how He's provided for me, even touched me emotionally and restored my soul. He has always filled my bucket! He has been my dearest and closest friend as long as I can remember. Each of my trials has a testimony

Whatever problem you are facing today that doesn't make sense—to which God has given you an answer that doesn't make sense—it is faith that will deliver you.

of triumph represented by a trophy. So as I pick up each trophy in my mind, I remember His goodness. As I do, I get more courageous about the difficulties I may be facing today. Faith begins to rise. I become even more expectant of His intervention and the power of possibility. Then it moves me to praise. I get emotionally engaged with Him.

Here, in my trophy room, it's just the two of us. I discover emotions of invincibility. I imagine myself indestructible. *I cannot fail. I cannot be defeated.* Surrounded by these trophies—the end result of my experiences of faith—I am encouraged to keep growing, to keep thriving, to keep living. What feels seemingly impossible in one moment can be overwhelmed by the power of possibility in the next. And as I leave my trophy room each time I visit, I glance back knowing I'll be back once again to put another trophy on the wall.

Each trophy represents real tests, trials and problems that I have encountered and overcome—just like Peter did: "These problems have come so that your faith may be proven genuine."

Whatever problem you are facing today that doesn't make sense—to which God has given you an answer that doesn't make sense—it is faith that will deliver you. The answer that doesn't make sense will make faith. But it is your assignment to live it out, to do what God has directed. Your situation may seem impossible, but He is the God of the power of possibility. Let Him walk you through—and eventually beyond—the situation that is testing your faith—and once again you will know it is always right to trust God and His Word again and again.

DON'T LET FAILURE DEFINE YOUR COURSE

Living this way is a commitment Missy and I made years ago, and we've been tested many times. In 1999, we left our comfort zone, working for a faith-filled ministry for more than 20 years, and began a ministry and a church. At 39 years old, at the height of our success, it didn't seem like the appropriate time to make such a move. But why not? Why not go out on top?

The answer that doesn't make sense will make faith.

In that season of transition, people said to us, "You've given the best days of your life to this ministry. You're leaders, and you're gonna walk away?"

I never walked away. I moved up. I knew what God had created me to do. I knew what I was hardwired to do. And despite the challenges, I have stayed my course. I have continued to grow…and allowed my faith to thrive.

I remember graciously listening to all of these kinds of comments, but on the inside I knew the best was yet to come. For a few years God had been talking to me, preparing me. He would get me up at 4 a.m. to talk. I journaled all He said—writing down wisdoms and strategies. So it wasn't surprising one day when I received a phone call from a gentleman I hadn't heard from in five years.

---

*Your situation may seem impossible, but He is
the God of the power of possibility.*

He was a minister who had endured hardship in the ministry. I listened to him tell 45-minutes-worth of ministry horror stories. The last bit of advice he gave me was: "Do everything you can not to go into full-time ministry."

This man did not know anything about my future plans. Remember what I said about the enemy influencing people to get to you? He spoke to me from his failures and was trying to convince me not to express my faith in God.

During that same period of time, Missy went to a local Barnes and Noble bookstore. In preparation for our future, she was accumulating research and material about the region where we were moving. The woman behind the cash register asked her why she was buying books on the panhandle of Texas.

Missy answered, "Well, we're considering moving to Amarillo."

"Ma'am," the woman said, "I used to live in Amarillo—and you don't want to move there. Do everything you can to not go there!" Because of her failures, she too tried to convince us not to go—not to even try!

When God speaks to you about doing something—the devil will show up through somebody else who has a victim mentality, who will attempt to talk you out of expressing your faith in God!

If you aren't watchful, people's sad stories will talk you out of doing the very things that are God's purpose for your life.

How many times have people prevented you from expressing your faith in God? Right at that moment is when we choose whether to succeed or abandon the dream God's given to us.

I don't know where you are today, whether you are on track or not. But if you're not, it's time to get back on the right course. The enemy has tried to sabotage your journey and contaminate your relationship with God. Don't let him succeed! Don't let failure—yours or others—define your course. God has a plan for you—and your faith is to thrive and take you there!

Sabotaging Our Future

I know I've talked a lot about my dad in this book, but I admire his journey. It was full of change and trials, but he always kept moving forward the best way he knew how—and he certainly knew faith.

I remember how, shortly after he was born again, he led our family toward a more extremist lifestyle. What I mean by this is a more religious lifestyle—not necessarily a more spiritual one.

Let Him walk you through—and eventually beyond—the situation that is testing your faith—and once again you will know it is always right to trust God and His Word again and again.

This was evident by the radical decisions he made: The TV went out on the curb for the trash truck to pick up. My mom and three sisters had to stop wearing jewelry and makeup. They had to wear their hair up in a bun, and the length of their dresses came way down. You know what I'm talking about!

165

When my dad got saved, he fell in love with God. He so wanted to please God. In his immaturity, when someone who had influence in his life began judging him and his family—condemning my dad from their own legalistic relationship with God—my dad followed. He was zealous and hungry for God. If something seemed right, he jumped on it. What was interesting is that his condemning friend used scripture to back up his influence: "Come out from them and be ye separate."[15] My dad's friend was convincing him to perform for God to win God's acceptance and approval.

Dad's friend, and the group in which he was associated, thought that for the most part, all denominations and churches displeased God. They questioned whether anyone who didn't attend their church would go to heaven. My mom and dad, in their innocent, pure pursuit of God, fell into this trap and took us four kids with them.

Even as a little boy, the rules, regulations, restrictions and restraints took the fun out of what was once a joyful, lively, relational pursuit of God! Everything became an obligation, a duty, and a ritual about trying not to displease God, to earn our way into heaven!

Our relationship with God is not about performance. It's about approaching God the right way through relationship.

Thank God, it didn't take long for their eyes to open. God showed my parents the truth—that there was no goodness, mercy, joy or love through this legalistic approach. They realized that the goodness of God leads all men to repentance—not the judgment of God![16]

I was overjoyed the day my parents returned to the place where their relationship with God began. Joy, life and fun filled our home.

All of the rituals, obligations and duties went out the window. And we started experiencing the goodness of God in our home once again.

The hair came down, the length of the dresses went up, and the girls loaded up with makeup and jewelry! As they say, "If the house needs painting, paint it!" We were a much better looking family painted!

> *It's the goodness of God that leads all men to repentance, because this is how God wants all men to see Him!*

Our relationship with God is not about performance. It's about approaching God the right way through relationship.

When Moses wanted to see God's face on Mt. Sinai, he asked. God answered, "No man can see my face and live, but I'll put you into a cave in this mountain…so when I pass by you can see My goodness." The first thing God wanted Moses to see of Himself was His goodness.

It's the goodness of God that leads all men to repentance, because this is how God wants all men to see Him! He wants you to know His goodness first and foremost—if for no other reason He wants to make a good first impression! After all, goodness is the motivation of all healthy relationships.

Jesus went about doing good.[17]

Why?

Because this is the first thing God wanted people to see about Him. He wanted the foundation of their relationship to be built on His goodness.

Some say: "Well, if you approach your relationship with God that way, you're just giving people a license to sin."

That is ridiculous! People don't' need a license to sin. They have been sinning for centuries without a license!

God is not into legalism—He's into relationship. The legalistic believer represents a hard, mean-spirited, judgmental and accusato-

---

As genuine believers, we are to approach God from the perspective and belief that "God is good, and He is good to me. God is doing good in my life."

---

ry, religious Christian. It's like they are a hammer, and when you're a hammer, everyone else looks like a nail, so you drive people through fear, control and manipulation!

As genuine believers, we are to approach God from the perspective and belief that "God is good, and He is good to me. God is doing good in my life. He wants good things to happen for me. What the devil means for harm, God is turning it for my good today! He's making good things happen in my life. And I'm to see the good in others."

When we have the right mindset about God and His approach to us, then we will have the correct emotions and feelings about Him—and ourselves. We were born into a kingdom of goodness to demonstrate His goodness to others.

Expressing our faith in everyday life is important especially in the life of today's new believer. As you've already realized, there is nothing that is for sure, except the goodness of God!

There are no for-sure, life-long relationships.

There are no for-sure jobs.

There is no risk-free anything.

There are no certainties.

In fact, faith doesn't grow in the environment of certainty. The only sure thing we are guaranteed is our relationship with God and our faith in Him. And the more we risk our lives by throwing ourselves into His kingdom, the greater our success, and the stronger our faith grows.

It seems impractical, maybe even impossible, at times to face all we do, but it's in the relational exchanges we have with Him, especially in trials, that the power of possibility is so real.

As we express our faith daily, it does something spectacular. It grows constantly instead of sporadically. The cycle of difficulty gets short-circuited. The season of feeling like "when it rains, it pours" suddenly ends—even when it feels it's been raining forever. The cycle of terminal unrelenting problems becomes a life of only sporadic and infrequent troubles.

> *When we have the right mindset about God and His approach to us, then we will have the correct emotions and feelings about Him— and ourselves.*

Yes, your life can look like this. Troubles can actually be unusual instead of the norm. Your faith can become the mountain that towers over your problems—and they can fade into insignificant difficulties.

Your daily expression of faith in God can create an unshakeable, unmovable fortress. By expressing your faith, you will not become another statistic. You'll beat the odds. You won't be a failure, but a winner.

When you trust God, He honors your faith. He backs your stand of faith, and the power of possibility changes everything!

CHAPTER 13

OUR CALL TO ACTION

WHATEVER HE TELLS YOU TO DO, DO IT!

"Meet the Pastor" was the theme as I shook hands with mothers, fathers, sisters and brothers. I kept noticing a tall man, standing at a distance watching my every move.

His eyes were fixed on me for 10-15 minutes. As the line of people grew shorter and shorter, he and his wife stepped to the end. By the time he got to me, he was in tears.

"I'm John (not his real name), this is my wife, and I'm an alcoholic, and I abuse my wife when I drink." By then, they were both crying uncontrollably. He concluded, "I'm done, I give up."

With his permission, I laid hands on him, and like a bird takes flight, it left him. Every desire—everything that drove him to it—gone. Months later, I saw him and his wife again. They were totally free, their lives restored, their marriage healed. That's the power of possibility.

I believed and practiced what Jesus said: "Lay hands on the sick and they will recover."[1] This was Jesus' call to action for every believer. I believed it, acted on it, and John got healed!

Before starting BelieversWay, I worked as the director of television for a successful, worldwide TV evangelist. Each workday morning, my staff gathered in our department for prayer and devotions before the busyness of our day began. I was notoriously known for having long devotions. I had a captive audience!

Doing what God says is imperative. "Whatever He tells you to do, do it." The potential in your miracle is waiting on the other side of your acting on it.

I'd wake up each morning not knowing a single thing I was going to say, but as I was driving to work, the Lord would give me just one phrase, one verse, one event, one experience. I'd teach a lesson on it…and all kinds of things would happen. I did that for years.

One morning a staff member came in who was frantic. She totally disturbed our devotions that day. So I just stopped everything, put my Bible down, and asked, "What's wrong?"

She didn't care that there were 35 people listening to what she was saying. "I'm just so tired of this car I'm driving. It's breaking down on me every day, and I just don't know what to do about it. I'm fed up with it!"

She was a single mother with a teenage daughter. Her life was one big busy schedule of going to work, dropping her daughter off at school, getting her to after-school activities, then to church on Wednesdays and Sundays. It was a life on the road—in a car!

I told her, "We're going to do something about that right now! Aren't we team?"

"Yes sir, we are!"

We all grabbed hands with one another and prayed: "In the Name of Jesus Christ of Nazareth, Father, we're asking you to bring her a car right now!" I prayed out everything the Holy Spirit gave me to pray, speak and pronounce over the situation including calling a car into her life. The team agreed in prayer with all I said, and we knew it was done.

Then I went right back to teaching.

That afternoon, a man who owned a used car company drove up in the parking lot of the TV building, walked through the front door, and said to the receptionist, "I don't know what you're going to think about me, in fact, you may think I'm crazy, but the Lord told me that there's someone here that needs a car. So here are the keys. Take it. Who is it anyway?"

Well, no one could say, "Well, it's me. Oh, that's mine! I was believing God for that, so it's my car."

Everyone knew whose it was because we prayed specifically for our friend that morning! Before sunset, she received the answer to her prayer. We released the power of possibility and she experienced it. It was out of that group of people that we forged a smaller prayer group of about eight to ten people. When serious issues were brought to our attention, like a friend with cancer, or a person with some other terrible crisis, we prayed. We began to document the people who were healed from cancer, diabetes, migraine headaches, and all kinds of problems. We prayed having ownership of the Name of Jesus. We released the power of possibility and they experienced it.

We answered a call to action—the same call to action that God assigns to all of us. We didn't keep what we knew to ourselves. We shared it. We acted on it—and the power of possibility grew.

WHAT HAS HE TOLD YOU TO DO?

Every time we answered a call to action, God responded—just like He did in the pages of the Bible. What has He called you to do?

God expects us to respond just like Jesus did. He is our example in story after story. Remember the wedding in Cana?[2]

Mary, the mother of Jesus, was hosting a wedding in Cana and the festivities were in full swing when someone told her they had run out of wine.

Stressed and concerned as to what to do next, Mary turned to Jesus and told Him in no uncertain terms, "I need a miracle—period." This was before Jesus had ever performed a public miracle.

She then turned to the caterers and said, "Do whatever He tells you."[3] We know from the story His time was not yet—meaning He wasn't ready to perform any miracles publicly. He said so. From the scriptures, we know He only did and said what His Father told Him to do. But on this day, His mother Mary moved God, who then moved Jesus through a call to action.

I'm sure these guys were expecting Jesus to hand them some money so they could rush to the store and get some more. But that's not what happened.

Jesus looked around the room and saw six stone jars. These were big jars—they were used for the Jewish ceremonial washings and could hold about 20 to 30 gallons each.

Jesus told the caterers, "Fill 'em up with water."[4]

Jesus called them into action.

So they did as He said.

Then He told them, "Now draw some out and take it to the master of the banquet."[5]

At this point, these guys are thinking, *What on earth is He doing? The master may have had a little wine, but he hasn't had that much! He's never going to be fooled with water. But Mary said do whatever Jesus told us…I sure hope He knows what He's doing!*

The master of the banquet tasted the water that had been turned into wine and loved it! He did not realize where it had come from, though the servants who had drawn the water knew. He called the bridegroom aside and said, "'Everyone brings out the choice wine first and then the cheaper wine after the guests have had too much to drink, but you have saved the best till now.' This, the first of His miraculous signs, Jesus performed in Cana of Galilee. He thus revealed His glory, and His disciples put their faith in Him."[6]

> *No matter how strange it sounds, do what God says do. Your action will release the power of possibility into your life.*

If the caterers had not acted on what Jesus asked them to do, the miracle would never have happened, the party would have been ruined, and Jesus' glory would not have been revealed. Again, listen to this call to action:

"Whatever He tells you to do, do it."

Doing what God says is imperative. "Whatever He tells you to do, do it." The potential in your miracle is waiting on the other side of your acting on it. No matter how strange it sounds, do what God says do. Your action will release the power of possibility into your life.

Remember the story when Jesus was out walking the shores of the Lake of Gennesaret, and He came upon Peter, who had been out fishing all night? Peter had just finished cleaning all of His nets and was about to head home. He slept during the day because the lake was so clear the fish could see the net. At night, when the nets were hidden in the darkness, was the only time it was possible to catch any fish. So, Peter was getting ready to head home and take a nap. Remember, Peter is a successful professional fisherman. This is how he has made his living.

Jesus interrupted that plan though and asked Peter if he would take the boat out from the shore. Once out on the water, Jesus turned to the multitudes who had been following Him and He preached for a while using the boat as His platform.

After He was done and they had returned to the shore, Jesus gave Peter a call to action, "Now, go out in the deep and go fishing."

I'm sure Peter must have thought this was a waste of time, because it didn't line up with the sequential order of his linear thinking. *That doesn't make any sense. No one in their right mind fishes during the day because it's pointless. Who ever heard of catching fish this time of day?*

> *When God calls you to action, many times, it's a moment in time that seems to have impossible results—a moment where you do something just because He says to.*

"Master, we've worked hard all night and haven't caught anything. But because you say so, I will let down the nets."[7]

It doesn't make any sense, "But because You say so...."

Peter let down his nets and caught the catch of a lifetime. There were so many fish in his nets that it began to break, so Peter had to call in reinforcements.

When God calls you to action, many times, it's a moment in time that seems to have impossible results—a moment where you do something just because He says to.

One of his buddies was nearby, so Peter called him over to take in part of the catch, but the catch was even more than two boats could manage, so their boats began to sink—in the middle of the day, when it should have been impossible to catch anything!

What would have happened if Peter hadn't answered this call to action? What if he had been content to rely on his own personal experience and logic?

He would have missed out on the catch of a lifetime! That's what would have happened! Just because it didn't make sense didn't mean it wasn't possible.

When God tells us to do something—whether it makes sense or not—we should do it, or we potentially could miss out on the power of possibility being released into our lives.

YOUR ACTION IS THE CATALYST

My dad told me a story once how God told him to do something that didn't make sense—but it made faith. He recounted how one day as he spent time with the Lord, the Lord told him, "I want you to give the $2,000 in your church's bank account to another ministry. Just send it to them."

When he looked at his ledger, it showed a balance of just a little over $2,000. I'm sure he thought of all the reasons why he couldn't do this. *It's Tuesday…we've got to pay bills…we've got payroll…and we've got things we've got to do here.*

I'm sure he told the Lord all the reasons why he couldn't do it. But when God tells you to do something, even though you'll have a thousand reasons why you can't do it, do what God tells you to do. Just do it anyway. God often will contradict our thinking. That's one of the ways I know it's God! It doesn't make sense—but it makes faith!

Since Dad had experienced success in this area before, he knew when God gave him direction, he was to do exactly as he heard. So he wrote a $2,000 check, and sent it to the ministry.

Several weeks later, a stranger walked into his church. He entered my dad's office where he was studying, and at the end of their conversation, after talking for 20-30 minutes, the man pulled out his checkbook and wrote the church a $40,000 check.

God will always call us to action because faith without action is dead. My dad responded to what he heard. His response was a catalyst for the power of possibility. He answered the call to action—and the reward of his faith was great.

YOU HAVE TO TRUST

When God gives us a call to action that doesn't make sense, things that seem impossible, it's important that we trust Him and do it anyway. Isaac in the Bible is a great example of living this.

During the second great famine that had struck the land of Canaan, people were desperate. They were running out of food and water and starvation was near. Isaac was considering taking his family to Egypt so they wouldn't starve. That was the logical thing to do. But the Lord appeared to him and gave him two calls to action.

The first was, "Don't leave this land."

The second was, "Stay here and sow seed in this time of famine."[8]

Who plants during a time of extreme drought and famine? It hadn't rained in ages, and the ground was dry and cracked. Any logical person knew that nothing could grow in those conditions. But Isaac trusted God, regardless of the circumstances, and acted on it. He knew that whatever God told him to do, he should do it.

"Isaac planted crops in that land and the same year reaped a hundredfold, because the Lord blessed him. The man became rich, and his wealth continued to grow until he became very wealthy. He had so many flocks and herds and servants that the Philistines envied him."[9]

Not only did Isaac grow enough food to feed himself and his family, he obviously had enough to sell and save other's lives, too.

Who would have ever thought that planting in a drought would work? No one! That was God's point. His plan wasn't designed to make sense—it was designed to create faith so the power of possibility would become reality.

In the early days of our first church, when we had only a hundred people attending, one Wednesday evening before service, the Lord said, "I want you to give everyone in the service tonight who needs finances a twenty-dollar bill."

> *God will always call us to action because*
> *faith without action is dead.*

Here was my call to action. Would I do it? Have you ever been in a church where a pastor did that?

I wrestled with it, then called Missy and told her about it. She went to the bank and got 15 twenty-dollar bills and put them in an envelope. I had three twenty-dollar bills in my pocket along with some ones and fives.

That night, 21 people came to the altar because they needed financial help. As Missy was assisting me, holding the envelope with 15 twenties, she whispered, "What are we going to do? We only have 15 twenty-dollar bills."

"Give me the envelope." I started down the line laying hands on people and sowing twenty-dollar bills.

I declared to each one, "I sow this twenty dollar bill into your life to produce financial increase." I kept shelling out twenties, and when I got to the 15th person, I was still passing out twenties! As I moved down the line, multiplication happened. I gave out exactly 21 twenty-dollar bills.

When God gives you a call to action, act on it.

That's not all to this story. There's more. One of the people in whom I sowed a twenty-dollar bill and prayed over was a visitor. I had instructed her, "Now put that with the rest of your money. There is an anointing for increase." Sure enough, she called us three months later and reported that $200,000 dollars unexpectedly had come into her life.

> *"For I know the plans I have for you,' declares the Lord, 'plans to prosper you and not to harm you, plans to give you hope and a future."*

I don't know how that happened to her, and I don't care really!

When we know God has a plan for each and every one of us… and every plan He has is good…and it is always far more than we could ever come up with on our own…then we can trust Him when He calls on us to act on His behalf.

"'For I know the plans I have for you,' declares the Lord, 'plans to prosper you and not to harm you, plans to give you hope and a future.'"[10]

"And we know He is able to do immeasurably more than all we ask or imagine, according to His power that is at work within us."[11]

Housed inside the plan of God for our lives is everything we need: our prosperity, our peace, our hope, and our future—and all better than anything we could ever ask or imagine! With God's plan will come initiatives and catalysts labeled "calls to action" that will set the wheels of His plan into perpetual motion.

I'm sure becoming wealthy wasn't even on Isaac's mind when he planted those seeds in that dry ground. His only concern at that very moment was to keep his family fed and alive.

God's plan is always so much more than just the here-and-now. He always has the future in mind, too, and it's better than we could even think to ask.

So, whatever He tells you to do, do it!

SEEDS OF FAITH YIELD HARVESTS FOR GENERATIONS

When I was a boy, I can remember many times that we needed money. During those times, I often watched my dad sit behind his desk and get out his checkbook. He would send checks to other pastors in town even though we could have used that money more than them.

My dad knew that the best thing he could do was to sow seed, even in our time of famine. It didn't make sense, but it made faith. Each time he did it, the power of possibility was released, and God would resource us and meet our need.

The harvest always came. Each and every seed Dad sowed always sent a harvest above anything we could have ever asked. Dad was so wise and faithful. Whether he knew it or not, he was not only sowing seeds of financial prosperity into our lives, but also he was sowing seeds of faith into mine.

Housed inside the plan of God for our lives is everything we need: our prosperity, our peace, our hope, and our future—and all better than anything we could ever ask or imagine!

Today, those seeds are what God explained to me as the power of possibility.

I am so thankful that my dad answered God's call and acted accordingly by doing what the Word says to do! If he hadn't, where would I be now? Where would my family be? BelieversWay would be an unrealized dream. And where would you be? This message is for you. This book is for you.

GO THE WAY OF GOD'S RESULTS, PLANS AND DREAMS

All too often though, people get focused on the problem that doesn't make sense, and when God speaks, He gives them a call to action that doesn't make sense either. When that happens, the problem grows bigger in their minds and makes an impossible situation seem even more impossible. Now they really have a problem. When they can't see past it, they start trying to bring God down to their level.

They start trying to convince God that instead of getting into motion on the basis of His call to action, that they should save the money, take a nap, go on vacation, head for the escape hatch, or reach for the easy button! But when they do that, they miss out on God's results and plans. Dreams are made under pressure.

> *God's plan is always so much more than just the here-and-now. He always has the future in mind, too, and it's better than we could even think to ask.*

I'm one of those types of people who have conversations with myself. I'll take a scripture in the Bible and compare my life to it. For instance Ephesians 3:20 says, "He is able to do exceedingly, abundantly, above all I can ask or think [great sounds good] according to the power at work in me."

Everything about that scripture was on God until He added "according to." That phrase changed everything. "According to the power at work in me."

The elevation of your life is determined by the size of you.

So here goes the dialogue…

How much power is in me?

How big am I anyway?

What is the size of my soul?

How vast is my attitude?

What capacity do I have inside me?

How much wisdom do I possess?

Because the elevation of my life is according to the size of me, the outcome of my life is determined by me. I can either limit the unlimited one—God—or I can maximize God's power by giving Him a whole me who doesn't restrict Him from doing anything or going anywhere with my life. I decided years ago to follow Jesus' example: "And Jesus increased in wisdom and stature, and in favor with God and men."[12]

Jesus had to grow?

Yes. Jesus grew in wisdom, stature and favor with God and man. And His growth created an unrestricted zone for God's power of possibility to circulate through Him. Jesus had potential placed in Him by God, but He had to grow His inner world—stature, wisdom and favor—to maximize His potential. Jesus was big. He went about doing good and healing all who were oppressed of the devil for God was with Him.[13]

The elevation of your life is determined by the size of you.

So, how do you carry yourself?

183

Can you carry your finances, marriage, and family?

Can you carry others outside of your own personal world?

How many people live off your life?

Can you walk into a hostile atmosphere where there is turmoil and confusion, change the environment, and leave peace and tranquility behind?

GOD WAS HERE

When I was a kid in school, my buddies and I, when we would go somewhere, liked to leave our mark, or signature. It read something like this: "Scott was here!"

When our inner world grows to a certain size, then the power of possibility is circulating through us, unhindered, unrestricted without restraint, and then we change the atmosphere. We leave behind God's mark: "God was here!"

This is how I have chosen to live my life.

He was anointed to preach, to heal, to deliver, to rescue. But instead of seeking a platform to be understood, He came to understand.

I remember years ago, Missy and I had a friend who was having a lot of dental work performed. At the time, I didn't know about it.

As the story goes, where the dentist had worked on one side of her mouth was the most painful thing she'd ever been through. When she was scheduled to get her teeth fixed on the other side, she and her husband asked us to "please pray."

Still, without knowing what was going on, I replied, "Absolutely." As I spoke, I heard these words come out of my heart: "This time it will be different. Don't be afraid."

I proceeded to pray and bring resistance to the pain. A few days later, she called: "It was just like you said. I didn't have one second of pain or discomfort."

God had left his mark. It read, "God was here."

GOD UNDERSTANDS YOU TODAY

If Jesus had to grow His life and faith, and not enter His earthly ministry until He was 30, then who do I think I am?

For decades, at each juncture in life, I had consistently asked the Lord, "When do you want me to go for my dream?"

Each time, the Lord said, "Wait and grow."

One afternoon, when I was 35 years old, I began to think, *Lord, I'm running out of time.*

The conversation went something like this: "Lord, I have a message to preach. I have a fire for this calling you've placed on my life."

Suddenly the Lord interrupted me and said, "Scott, take the fire inside you and turn it on you. Burn yourself up first, so when I send you out, you won't get in the way."

For the next four years, I simply turned up the heat.

Jesus' life tells us that He spent 30 years accumulating information about humanity to understand us—you and me. Imagine 30 years with pent up power, 30 years with mountain-moving faith, 30 years with the ability to perform profound miracles, 30 years without giving wisdom—even though He was wiser than anyone—30 years without preaching the message God sent Him to preach.

Luke recorded what He had to say: "The spirit of the Lord is upon me for he has anointed me to preach."[14]

He was anointed to preach, to heal, to deliver, to rescue. But instead of seeking a platform to be understood, He came to understand. Do you know how hard that is? Maybe this will help. Have you ever had the answer to the question, but everyone assumed you didn't? All the while inside, you were shouting, "I know, I know, I know."

That's how the Son of God must have felt. But He wouldn't open His mouth, because He came to listen, and observe, to understand humanity in a way no one ever had, nor ever will again. He bridged the gap that existed between God and man. And from a position of understanding us, He then explained us to ourselves. This is the approach of someone on a search and rescue team. He has located you, locked on to you, and searched you out. God understands you today.

Whatever God tells you to do—whether it seems impossible or unreasonable—do it! God didn't design it to make sense—He designed it to release the power of possibility into your life!

Like Jesus, I have to set the thermostat of my life on grow, so that like Him, others can live off my life. I change the environment wherever I go. The atmosphere is altered drastically for the good, because I release the power of possibility. I'm a carrier of God's "goodness virus" and I leave it behind everywhere I go. I leave His mark, His signature… "God was here."

There's a reason why God's thoughts and ways are above ours. It's because He gets results that are greater than any result we could ever get on our own! If He did things the way we do, He would get the same results we get—and frankly, that's just not good enough!

When God calls you to action—do it—and experience His results. He has a purpose for every Word that comes out of His mouth.

Whatever God tells you to do—whether it seems impossible or unreasonable—do it! God didn't design it to make sense—He designed it to release the power of possibility into your life!

ENDNOTES

All scripture is from the *New International Version*
unless noted in the following references.

CHAPTER 1

[1] *Blessed Assurance,* written by Fanny Crosby, 1873, Brooklyn, NY.

[2] *Jesus Is The Sweetest Name I Know,* originally *He Keeps Me Singing,*
written by Luther B. Bridgers, 1911.

[3] 2 Kings 6, *The Message*

[4] Daniel 6

[5] Exodus 14

[6] 1 Kings 17

[7] 1 Kings 17:12-14

[8] 1 Kings 17:15-16

[9] 2 Corinthians 4:18

[10] John 4:24

[11] 1 Thessalonians 5:23

[12] Proverbs 18:14

[13] Zechariah 4:6

[14] Matthew 6:10

[15] Mark 16:18

[16] John 3:16

CHAPTER 2

1. Proverbs 3:5
2. Mark 5:30-34
3. Romans 10:17
4. Ephesians 6:12
5. Genesis 8:22, *New King James Version*
6. Hebrews 11:6
7. 1 Corinthians 6:19
8. Romans 8:11
9. 3 John 2
10. Hebrew 11:3
11. Matthew 18:3

CHAPTER 3

1. Matthew 24:10
2. Matthew 22:38-39
3. Luke 17:4-5, *New King James Version*
4. Matthew 6:14-15
5. 1 Corinthians 13:8
6. 2 Timothy 1:12
7. Lamentations 3:22-24
8. James 2:13
9. James 1:5

CHAPTER 4

1. Psalm 18:23
2. Psalm 22:3
3. John 10:10
4. Matthew 11:28-30, *The Message*

5 Matthew 11:29-30

6 Romans 8:19

7 Hebrews 11:1

8 Romans 12:3

9 Hebrews 11:1

10 Proverbs 4:7

11 Romans 12:3

12 Hosea 4:6

13 Proverbs 4:7

14 Proverbs 4:7

15 Luke 2:52

16 1 Corinthians 10:13

17 Jeremiah 29:11

18 Isaiah 54:17

19 Colossians 3:3, *New King James Version*

20 John 15:7, *New King James Version*

21 Psalm 91:1, *New King James Version*

22 Colossians 2:10

23 1 John 4:16

24 Habakkuk 2:4

25 Hebrews 11:6

26 Mark 16:18

CHAPTER 5

1 Ephesians 2:2, *The Amplified Bible*

2 Proverbs 18:21

3 Proverbs 20:5, *New American Standard*

4 Luke 4:18, *New King James Version*

5 Matthew 18:18, *New King James Version*

6 Romans 8:31

[7] Acts 16:22-26, *The Message*

[8] Matthew 11:28

[9] Song of Solomon 2:1

[10] In 1 Peter 5:6

[11] James 4:7

[12] Joel 3:10

[13] Mark 11:23, *New King James Version*

[14] Genesis 8:22

[15] Proverbs 24:10, *The Message*

[16] John 16:33

[17] John 16:33, *The Message*

[18] Ephesians 6:12, *New King James Version*

[19] Revelation 12

[20] Romans 5:3-4

[21] Romans 8:28, *New King James Version*

[22] Romans 4:20

[23] James 2:21-22, *The Amplified Bible*

CHAPTER 6

[1] 1 Corinthians 6:9

[2] Acts 10:38

[3] Romans 12:21

[4] John 14:30

[5] Proverbs 4:7

[6] Genesis 37 and the following chapters.

[7] Romans 1:20

[8] John 1:1-3, *New King James Version*

[9] John 1:14, *New King James Version*

[10] John 4

[11] John 4:28-29

12 1 Corinthians 14:33
13 1 Peter 1:8
14 John 4:41-42
15 Matthew 11:28-30

CHAPTER 7

1 Matthew 15:13
2 Psalm 34:1
3 Romans 10:17, *New King James Version*
4 2 Corinthians 5:17
5 Proverbs 11:24, *King James Version*
6 Proverbs 11:24, *The Message*
7 Mark 16:20
8 Jeremiah 1:12
9 Isaiah 55:11

CHAPTER 8

1 Matthew 19:24
2 Hebrews 12:1
3 John 10:1-3
4 Romans 12:2, *The New Living Translation*
5 Luke 14:16-21, *The Message*
6 Proverbs 16:9
7 James 4:8
8 Luke 6:38
9 Psalm 37:23
10 Mark 16:17
11 Matthew 16:4
12 Acts 16:6-10, *New Living Translation*
13 Acts 16:6

14 Mark 6:11

15 Psalm 37:23-24

16 Philippians 3:12-13

17 1 Corinthians 4:2, *The Amplified Bible*

18 Proverbs 28:20, *New American Standard Bible*

19 Proverbs 10:22

CHAPTER 9

1 Romans 11:29

2 Romans 10:14, *New King James Version*

3 Joshua 6

4 Romans 10:14

5 James 2:17

6 Isaiah 30:18-20, *The Message*

7 Matthew 13:54-58

8 Joshua 6:20-21

9 Romans 10:14

CHAPTER 10

1 Isaiah 55:8-11

2 Romans 12:2

3 Matthew 6:33

4 Romans 11:29

5 Proverbs 29:18

6 1 Corinthians 9:24

7 Hebrews 12:1

8 James 1:6

9 Luke 6:47-49, *The Amplified Bible*

CHAPTER 11

1. 1 John 4:4
2. Romans 10:9
3. Revelation 12:10, *New Living Translation*
4. Isaiah 54:17, *New King James Version*
5. Luke 4:29
6. Luke 4:42
7. Romans 8:31
8. Ephesians 4:15
9. Hebrews 12:1
10. Romans 8:1
11. 1 Corinthians 2:16
12. Second Corinthians 4:17-18

CHAPTER 12

1. Romans 10:17
2. Hebrews 11:8
3. Ephesians 5:1, *New King James Version*
4. Isaiah 11:3, *The Amplified Bible*
5. First Peter 1:6-7
6. Nehemiah 4-6
7. Nehemiah 4:17
8. Daniel 3:28
9. Romans 8:28
10. 1 Peter 1:7
11. Matthew 14:26-30
12. Matthew 14:31
13. 1 John 5:4
14. Matthew 15:14
15. 2 Corinthians 6:17

16 Romans 2:4

17 Acts 10:38

CHAPTER 13

1 Mark 16

2 John 2

3 John 2:5

4 John 2:7, my paraphrase

5 John 2:8

6 John 2:8-11

7 Luke 5:5

8 Genesis 26:2-3, my paraphrase

9 Genesis 26:12-14

10 Jeremiah 29:11

11 Ephesians 3:20

12 Luke 2:52, *New King James Version*

13 Acts 10:38

14 Luke 4:18

APPENDIX I

HOW TO RECEIVE UNDERSTANDING

Proverbs 2:2   *"Apply thine heart...."*

Proverbs 2:3   *"Cry out..."*

Proverbs 2:4   *"Seek and search for it...."*

Proverbs 2:6   *"Listen to God...."*

Proverbs 5:1   *"Bow thine ear to my...."*

Proverbs 7:4   *"Treat it as a family...."*

Proverbs 15:32   *"Hear reproof...."*

Proverbs 4:7-Proverbs 8:1-36

Proverbs 16:16; 22

Ephesians 1:7-8

APPENDIX II

CHARACTERISTICS OF A MAN OR WOMAN OF UNDERSTANDING

Proverbs 2:9 — *Righteousness, judgment, equity, every good path*

Proverbs 3:4 — *Favor and understanding go hand and hand*

Proverbs 3:5 — *Does not allow own natural reasoning to overtake the knowledge of God (Word)*

Proverbs 3:16 — *Length of days, riches and honor*

Proverbs 3:17 — *Pleasantness, peace*

Proverbs 4:8 — *Promotion, bring to thee honor*

Proverbs 6:32 — *A man who commits adultery destroys himself*

Proverbs 9:6 — *Forsake the foolish*

Proverbs 9:10 — *Fears the Lord*

Proverbs 10:13 — *Wisdom is found on his lips...*

Proverbs 10:23	*Has wisdom, 14:33; 17:24*
Proverbs 11:12	*Holds his tongue, peace, 17:28 shuts his lips*
Proverbs 12:11	*Does not follow after vain people*
Proverbs 14:6	*Knowledge comes easy*
Proverbs 14:29	*Patience, slow to wrath*
Proverbs 15:21	*Walks uprightly, straight course*
Proverbs 17:27	*Excellent spirit, and even tempered*
Proverbs 19:8	*Prosperous*

About the Author

Scott Johnson is the founder, along with his wife, Missy, of BelieversWay Ministries, which includes BelieversWay Church, which has two locations in Amarillo and Midland, Texas, and the Christian TV show, *BelieversWay With Scott and Missy*.

Scott began in ministry by growing up in it as a pastor's son, then attending Rhema Bible Training Center, Tulsa, Oklahoma, in 1979, and later working for Kenneth Copeland Ministries, along with Missy, for more than 20 years, before beginning BelieversWay in 1999.

BelieversWay With Scott and Missy began in 2008, and airs weekdays on dish, DirectTV, and CTN around the world, as well as on **www.believersway.tv**.

Scott's passion is to take the message of BelieversWay—building each generation to reach the next, through the power of relationship—to today's believer with messages of faith and wisdom. He does this through preaching, teaching on television, mentoring others, writing books, and recording audio study series.

He and Missy, who is Gloria Copeland's sister, have three sons and live in Amarillo, Texas.

MORE FROM SCOTT JOHNSON

What's Got You?

Book 030910BK $5

Ever wonder why you are succeeding so much in one area of your life and failing miserably in another—all at the same time? What area of your life is not working right—finances, relationships, career? In this enlightening book, Scott answers these questions, and shares powerful revelation concerning the "attachments" in our lives—the associations we have with people, organizations, or even material things.

Clear the Mechanism— Silencing the Noise of Life

Book 1009BK.. $5

Until we learn to clear the mechanism, our lives will be riddled with regretful decisions, failed plans and missed opportunities. Learn how to *Clear the Mechanism* so you can rest assured that you are hearing the desires of God for your life, as well as for those within your sphere of influence. You can think clearly and make sound, positive decisions.

Transition

2 CD audio series   051709CDPK $10

Have you ever wished you had a built-in GPS system that would help you navigate through the changes and transitions in life? Have you relocated from one city to another? Bought a new house? Changed schools or jobs? You were in transition. In this series, Scott Johnson shares the 5 things we should do and the 5 things we must not do during transition.

Restoring the Lost Years

4 CD audio series   010310CD $20

Setbacks in life can be disheartening. And trying to make up for lost time is often over-whelming. Explore the depths of God's good-ness in a series that reveals His way of restoring anything you've ever lost. Learn how you can have twice as much as before!

VENT

3 CD audio series   031410CD $15

Stop blowing off steam and start blowing down barriers that keep you from success. Turn your frustrations into stepping-stones to your next promotion from God, as you learn to embrace the very pressures of life that can help you reach your fullest potential.

Your Nothing Is Something

3 CD audio series   080303CD.................$15

Look around. Is your life full of things you didn't expect? Discover how to up-root all the things you don't want in your life and replant them with all the goodness of God you do want. Take charge and you'll find the success you long for.

Courage For Change

4 CD audio series and magnet
083009CDS $20

Nothing stays the same forever except for God's nature. Times are changing—politically, socially, financially—there is change around every corner, and we can expect more to come. In this faith-building, courage-increasing series, Scott will teach you how to uncover the potential God has placed in you, and embrace change as an opportunity. You will learn that change often brings fear along for the ride, but we are called to be a people of faith—not fear! God's stability gives us the ability to stay the steady course and build *Courage for Change*.

CONTACT US

BELIEVERSWAY MINISTRIES
P.O. Box 20120
Amarillo, Texas 79114-0120
806-463-7284

BELIEVERSWAY CHURCH AMARILLO
6201 Canyon Drive, Suite 200
Amarillo, Texas 79110
806-463-7284

BELIEVERSWAY CHURCH MIDLAND
4400 N. Midland Drive, Suite 400
Midland, Texas 79707
432-689-7284

BELIEVERSWAY.TV
BelieversWay With Scott and Missy
PO Box 20120
Amarillo, Texas 79114-0120

Prayer Center 806-367-7096
Product Orders 866-333-7284

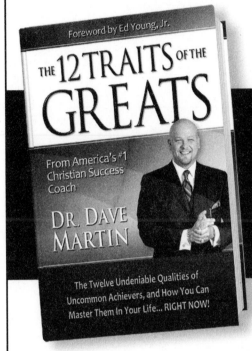

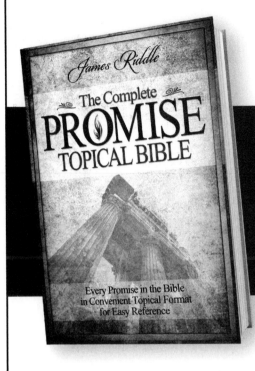

Fast. Easy. Convenient.

For the latest Harrison House product information and author news, look no further than your computer. All the details on our powerful, life-changing products are just a click away. New releases, E-mail subscriptions, testimonies, monthly specials—find it all in one place. Visit harrisonhouse.com today!

harrisonhouse

The Harrison House Vision

Proclaiming the truth and the power

Of the Gospel of Jesus Christ

With excellence;

Challenging Christians to

Live victoriously,

Grow spiritually,

Know God intimately.